Mothers' Work and Children's Lives

Mothers' Work and Children's Lives

Low-Income Families after Welfare Reform

Rucker C. Johnson
Ariel Kalil
Rachel E. Dunifon
with Barbara Ray

2010

W.E. Upjohn Institute for Employment Research
Kalamazoo, Michigan

Library of Congress Cataloging-in-Publication Data

Johnson, Rucker C.
Mothers' work and children's lives : low-income families after welfare reform / Rucker C. Johnson, Ariel Kalil, Rachel E. Dunifon with Barbara Ray.
p. cm.
Includes bibliographical references and index.
ISBN-13: 978-0-88099-356-2 (pbk. : alk. paper)
ISBN-10: 0-88099-356-1 (pbk. : alk. paper)
ISBN-13: 978-0-88099-358-6 (hardcover : alk. paper)
ISBN-10: 0-88099-358-8 (hardcover : alk. paper)
1. Low-income mothers—United States—Social conditions. 2. Child care—United States. 3. Public welfare—United States. I. Kalil, Ariel. II. Dunifon, Rachel E. (Rachel Elizabeth) III. Title.
HQ759.J65 2010
362.5'5610973—dc22
2009048131

Cover design by Alcorn Publication Design.
Index prepared by Diane Worden.
Printed in the United States of America.
Printed on recycled paper.

For Sheldon Danziger, our mentor and friend.

Contents

Figures

Tables

Acknowledgments

We are grateful for the support of many organizations and individuals who helped create and lead the Women's Employment Study (WES). Sandra Danziger, the principal investigator of the WES, deserves special recognition for her leadership. The survey development and the collection and analysis of the data were supported by numerous funders, including the Charles Stewart Mott Foundation, the Joyce Foundation, the John D. and Catherine T. MacArthur Foundation, the Substance Abuse Policy Research Program of the Robert Wood Johnson Foundation, the Annie E. Casey Foundation, the National Institute of Mental Health (R24 MH51363), the Office of the Assistant Secretary for Health and Human Services, and the University of Michigan Office of the Vice-President for Research. Postdoctoral training fellowships from the National Institute of Child Health and Human Development supported Kalil (F32 HD08145-01) and Dunifon (F32 HD08627-01) during the early years of the WES.

We are enormously grateful for the efforts of the data collection team from the Survey Research Center at the Institute for Social Research (University of Michigan), who ensured that our data are of the highest quality. Bruce Medbury was the survey manager for the first four waves of data collection, and Eva Leissou managed the final wave of data collection. Bruce in particular spent many long hours with us at the Poverty Research and Training Center, explaining with unflagging patience how to craft the survey instrument. The interviewing staff at the Institute for Social Research conducted the interviews with the highest degree of professionalism. We also thank Margaret Hudson, Sarah Marsh, Andreas Pape, and Patrick Wightman for excellent assistance with the data. We would like to extend a special thanks to our colleague Kristin Seefeldt for her generosity in sharing data from her qualitative interviews with WES participants. These data have greatly enriched the quantitative analyses that are the primary focus of this book. We are also extremely grateful for the work of Barbara Ray, whose writing and editing skills were invaluable.

Finally, we would like to thank the women who participated in the Women's Employment Study. Year after year, they agreed to share their personal stories, ranging from the setbacks of losing a job to the joys of raising children. We learned from them, and it is our hope that, through our analysis and discussion of their experiences, others will as well.

1
The Road to Welfare Reform

In December 1994, as the welfare reform bill was working its way through Congress, Jason DeParle, author of *American Dream* (2004) and longtime *New York Times* poverty reporter, wrote an article for the *New York Times Sunday Magazine* about a single mother of four juggling a low-wage job, poverty, and the daily strain of life on the margins (DeParle 1994). It was a prescient profile in many ways.

Mary Ann Moore, at age 33, was proud of herself. Although she'd had her first child as a teenager and spent the next 14 years on and off welfare, she was now on the right road. Every day, hours before the sun rose, she would drag herself off the couch that served as her bed, roust her kids, feed and dress them, and pile them into their beater of a car to drive the 11 miles to her mother's home. The children grew accustomed to the routine. After kissing them goodbye at her mother's apartment, Moore would head to her job in the kitchen at a homeless shelter, clocking in at 6:00 a.m. There she worked hard, putting in 52 hours a week, feeding 100 homeless people each day, and sometimes clocking two 13-hour shifts per week. Her toil barely paid the bills, but she felt better working than receiving welfare.

The story of Moore's life was, to many, a tale of the American way: work hard, take responsibility for yourself, be a role model for your children. Moore was doing that in spades.

Moore was also the vision policymakers in Washington in the early 1990s had for all women relying on welfare. As Bill Clinton himself said in the run-up to reform, "Work organizes life. It gives structure and discipline to life . . . It gives a role model to children." He was thinking then of Lillie Harden, a former welfare recipient in Arkansas who, when asked what she liked best about being off welfare, had said, "When my boy goes to school and they say, 'What does your mama do for a living?' he can give them an answer" (Safire 1997; U.S. Government Printing Office 1997).

When DeParle's story went to print in 1994, the rumbles of welfare reform were picking up steam. Although a number of important changes would be put into place in 1996, a set of gradual changes to the welfare program had in fact begun with the Family Support Act of 1988, which included, among other things, fewer work exemptions to mothers with ever younger children (see Haskins [2006] for a thorough account of welfare reform).[1] In 1992, then-candidate Clinton had campaigned on "ending welfare as we know it," and his advisers had been struggling since his inauguration to craft a welfare reform plan to which everyone could agree. The reform they were proposing centered on jobs and making work pay more than welfare by expanding the Earned Income Tax Credit (EITC), ensuring universal health coverage, and subsidizing child care costs. It also sought to transform the welfare system from a check-writing institution to one that sent a clear message: "Two years and you work."[2] The centerpiece was a mandate that recipients spend two years maximum on education and training followed by a job, either in the private sector, or if no private-sector job were available, in a meaningful public-sector job (Ellwood and Piven 1996).[3] The early version of the bill said nothing of lifetime limits, block grants, or the other mandates that eventually made their way into the reform bill.

Even though polls were showing that the country was solidly behind welfare reform, several aspects of the proposed reform were a difficult sell, mostly to fellow Democrats. The two-year requirement was alarming to many, and others thought the bill was simply too punitive. Politics and the timing of the bill also came into play. More important, money was tight, and preparing welfare recipients for jobs was much more expensive than just sending them a check every month. The country was running a significant budget deficit at the time, and no one could muster the votes to raise taxes in support of welfare and the poor. As the summer of 1994 drew to a close, a solid direction for welfare reform had still not materialized.

Of course, few could have predicted the events of that fall. With Newt Gingrich leading the charge, Republicans swept both houses of Congress, taking firm control of the reins. With that, Republicans were now poised to push through their own welfare reform proposals.

THE IDEOLOGICAL DIVIDE ON HELPING THE POOR

Those proposals, in fact, had been simmering for nearly a decade. Back in the mid-1980s, Ronald Reagan created potent images of "welfare queens" driving Cadillacs. The conservative base of the party, in fact, argued that welfare *caused* poverty by dulling poor women's motivation to work hard and lift themselves up. At about the same time, Charles Murray was publishing his "thought experiment" in *Losing Ground* (1984), the controversial book that would become the foundation of the Republican proposals for reforming welfare.[4] In that book, Murray laid out the perverse incentives built into welfare as he saw it with a fictional couple, Phyllis and Harold. Prior to the current welfare policies, Phyllis and Harold would have married after discovering Phyllis was pregnant, and Harold would have gone to work. However, with welfare in place, Phyllis and Harold shun both marriage and work and instead live off the welfare check that Phyllis now gets. They were, he said, acting rationally given the government assurance of cash assistance.

Following the same line of argument, other conservatives claimed that women were having more children so they could receive bigger welfare checks. Still others argued that welfare reform was the cause of teen pregnancy. If a young woman sees a safety net under her, they argued, there is no reason not to jump. Welfare, said Jason Turner, a key state-level player in reform, creates "enforced idleness that is responsible for much (though not all) of the decay in the social and family fabric" (Danziger 1997).[5] Mickey Kaus, the author of another influential book at the time, *The End of Equality* (1992) called welfare the "underclass culture's life support system."

Murray and his fellow conservatives were tapping into a sentiment in the American public that women on welfare were lazy, cheating the system, and in many respects were "to blame for so much that was wrong with America" (Piven, Hallock and Morgen 2002). The problem with the current policies, as Murray and others saw it, could be traced directly to a long line of liberal thinking about social problems. As Murray (1984) put it: "What emerged in the mid-1960s was an almost unbroken intellectual consensus that the individualist explanation of poverty was altogether outmoded and reactionary. Poverty was not a consequence of indolence or vice. It was not the just desserts of people who didn't try hard enough. It was produced by conditions that had nothing to do with individual virtue or effort. Poverty was not the fault of the individual but of the system" (p. 29).

Liberal scholars and others had long argued that families struggled in poverty not because of personal behavior, but because of larger, "structural" conditions that created an uneven playing field. The economy, for example, demanded higher skills, yet urban schools were failing to educate children. Wages had been stagnant for low-skilled workers since the late 1970s, and males, particularly African American males, had been hard hit by the slump. As investment and businesses left the inner city, jobs left with them, and inner-city unemployment rose to high levels. Many men became discouraged and dropped out of the job market, living with their girlfriends or mothers for support. Others turned to underground, sometimes illegal, markets to earn a living. Increasingly they were imprisoned.

These trends depleted the marriage pool of men, which scholars argue has contributed to the declining marriage rate in the urban African American community. Men with few prospects for employment, either because of a prison record or other reasons, are not attractive marriage partners in many women's eyes, as William Julius Wilson chronicled in *The Truly Disadvantaged* (1987). Yet, although marriage rates were on the decline, childbearing was not. Some might ask why women would not postpone childbearing knowing the toll that poverty imposes on children. The reason, as Edin and Kefalas (2005) find, lies in the response commonly offered by low-income urban women: "Wait for what?" Kefalas (2007) notes, "For a woman with a high school diploma, the $7-an-hour job she can land at [age] 18 is the same $7-an-hour job she'll be holding at 28."

Remedying these structural contributors to poverty, liberals argued, called for investing in job development, economic development, education and job training, and neighborhoods, while leaving a strong safety net in place. But Robert Rector of the conservative Heritage Foundation summed it up for many conservatives when he said in an online debate in 1997 that those ideas "sound an awful lot like spending more on things that have failed in the past . . . Our nation has since invested more than $6 trillion in fighting the war on poverty—and virtually every social problem has gotten worse, not better" (Rector 1997).

THE NEW WELFARE BILL

The result of this wrangling was a bill that passed in the Republican House only to be softened somewhat by the Senate in September 1995, but with some additional restrictions on immigrant eligibility. Clinton ultimately vetoed that bill and sent it back for compromise. The result was the 1996 Personal Responsibility and Work Opportunity Reconciliation Act (PRWORA). Its most striking feature was the abolishment of the guarantee for the poor of a welfare safety net. No longer was cash assistance an entitlement. Equally important were the work requirements in exchange for welfare (the "two years and you work" requirement) and five-year lifetime time limits on receipt of the newly named cash assistance program, Temporary Assistance for Needy Families (TANF).

Under the new law, a woman could only receive welfare for a cumulative total of 60 months, after which she was barred from returning to welfare. The law required states to have 50 percent of their TANF caseload in the workforce, and it required them to have 90 percent of two-parent families in the workforce. Going forward, states would receive a credit for further caseload declines. Specifically, the credit reduced the work participation rate by the percentage that the state reduced its overall caseload in the prior fiscal year compared with its caseload in 1995. Originally, states were not required to include families who were funded by separate state funds in these calculations.

Work requirements also specified that single parents were required to work at least 20 hours a week in 1997, rising to 30 hours a week by 2000. A key impetus for these work requirements, in addition to ending what many saw as long-term dependency, was the belief that work, through the order, routine, and income that it injected into family life, would ultimately benefit children. Mothers who did not work and relied instead on welfare, many argued, were not good role models for their children. Or as Rector (1997) put it, "Welfare costs a lot and generates dependence and illegitimacy, both of which are harmful to children's development."

Finally, to signal that it meant business, the federal program stipulated that those who failed to abide by the new rules were to be sanctioned by reducing the amount of their welfare check for each infraction. The carrot to this stick was the ability of states to "disregard" a larger share of earnings before reducing an individual's welfare check.

Under the new law, states were also allowed much more flexibility to manage their own cash assistance program, with some added risk. Rather than a federal stream of funding that rose or fell depending on caseloads, the new funding was a lump sum (block grants) based on a state's welfare spending between 1992 and 1996. If caseloads declined, the leftover money was theirs to use as needed for child care programs or even to plug other holes in state budgets. However, if caseloads rose, they had to make do with the set amount of funding.[6]

The new rules were flexible in other ways as well. Under the law, states must abide by the general requirements outlined in PRWORA, but they could be more or less strict on their own dime. For example, 24 states have imposed a time limit that results in complete termination of benefits at the end of 60 months of welfare receipt; 19 states have time limits that are shorter than 60 months. But, 8 states have no time limits on the receipt of cash assistance or provide indefinite benefits for the child portion of the case (Zedlewski et al. 2007). Some states imposed strict sanctions for not following the welfare rules, whereas others created more generous incentives to make work pay more than welfare. Other states shortened their "two years and you work" time limit and encouraged women to enter the workforce quickly. This "work first" approach was based on the philosophy that women with few skills or education would be better off learning those skills on the job than in a classroom.

Ultimately, the new welfare bill gave states what they had been clamoring for—independence to design a welfare program that reflected the conditions in their state. The new law also allowed the federal government to send a clear message: welfare is no longer an entitlement but a temporary support on the road to work. Wiped clean was the original intent of the program in the 1930s—to support single mothers who had been abandoned by a breadwinning man. Women were required to take personal responsibility for their livelihoods and join the country's ethos of work and self-sufficiency.

THE RESPONSE: WHAT ABOUT THE CHILDREN?

The push-back on the proposed bill was staunch, and at times hyperbolic. Critics of the bill were especially alarmed for the 1.1 million children that the Department of Health and Human Services estimated would be pushed into poverty by the loss of a safety net. The debate on the Hill and in the media was heated. Another Democratic Senator Daniel Patrick Moynihan famously claimed that children would be sleeping on the street grates and that there would be "scenes of social trauma such as we haven't known since the cholera epidemics" (DeParle 1994). Senator Edward Kennedy, prior to passage of the 1995 Senate bill, described it as "legislative child abuse" (Toner 1995).

Writing in an *Atlantic Monthly* online forum in 1997, one year into reform, Peter Edelman, a Clinton Administration welfare reformer who resigned when passage of the 1996 legislation was inevitable, said: "What we've now got instead is . . . a totally untried, underfinanced, and most important, undefined forced march of poor children out onto the high wire without a safety net" (Edelman 1997). He also predicted more homelessness, more family violence, more child abuse, more crime, more malnutrition, more drug abuse, and increased infant mortality.

An initial supporter of reform, Mary Jo Bane, former assistant secretary for the Administration for Children and Families in the Department of Health and Human Services, was also worried about the potential negative effects on children. Children, she said, would suffer from lack of supervision and appropriate discipline from parents who were away from home for long hours without the ability to provide good substitute care. "For some, abandonment or serious abuse or neglect will result. For others, the effects may show up in poor school performance and antisocial behavior" (Bane 1997, p. 49). Bane also saw the reformed child welfare system as ill equipped to handle the flood of children who would likely be in danger of abuse or neglect in the homes of struggling mothers who had lost their welfare benefits. She, too, resigned.

The prospect of a negative impact on children was not confined to Democrats. One of the earliest versions of the bill allowed states to use block grants to establish orphanages in stark recognition, as Mary Jo Bane pointed out in her essay on the foibles of the proposed reforms, "of the fact that some families would be denied assistance entirely and that not all parents would successfully meet the challenges of the new requirements" (Bane 1997, p. 52).

Finally came the warning of a "race to the bottom." With block grants to the states and few strings attached, some warned that states could do anything they wanted with their welfare programs, including nothing at all. Given that the remaining recipients were most likely those with the highest barriers to employment, including limited education, fragile mental health, and substance abuse or alcohol dependencies (Danziger et al. 2000), it would be less costly for states to push them off completely than to prepare them for jobs. The government spent approximately $5,000 per family annually under the current system. Creating a job for a mother and supplying child care would more than double that expense (DeParle 2004). Perhaps Bane had these families in mind when she warned that the loss of AFDC may be felt most in housing, with increased eviction, more doubling up, more moves, more crowding, and more violence-prone relationships.

These warnings were not plucked from the sky. Researchers have long explored the potential effects of working among single-mother families. A key question has always been one of time. More work means less time with children. Mothers who work long hours may have less time to provide emotional support, monitor their children's behavior, or foster the child's involvement in activities in school or in the community. They may also be tired and stressed, which can strain parenting. However, some evidence suggests that working mothers simply partition their days differently, cutting back on sleep and other tasks while continuing to devote the same "quality time" with their children (Bianchi 2000). Mary Ann Moore, for example, referred to her few hours of sleep as "cat naps," catching it where she could. Chase-Lansdale et al. (2003) have confirmed this idea by finding no reduction in time with children among low-income mothers leaving welfare for work.

There is also the issue of mothers' mental health and positive parenting. Unstable work or fluctuating work hours in a menial job can be stressful for anyone, let alone single parents, who frequently live in isolated neighborhoods with a long commute, often on public transportation, and whose child care is often unreliable (McLoyd et al. 1994). This added strain could increase the probability of mental health problems such as depression, which can make it hard for mothers to parent effectively (Kessler 1997). Similarly stressful is job loss or a string of jobs, which can be emotionally defeating. Some women faced with this uphill climb may turn to alcohol or drugs to relieve the stress (Catalano et al. 1993). Finally, job loss, nonstandard hours, and stressful, menial work can take a physical toll on mothers, which can impair the quality or quantity of time with children (Presser 2004).

As Bane argues, income instability (without the safety net of welfare) may cause some families to double up or send them on a nomadic journey from apartment to apartment (Bitler, Gelbach, and Hoynes 2006). If such doubling-up arrangements help families make ends meet financially, and if grandmothers help provide quality care for young children while mothers work, this could be a good thing. Indeed, some studies have shown positive impacts for low-income children when grandmothers live with them (DeLeire and Kalil 2002). On the other hand, if doubling up means forming households with other men, children could suffer, given that studies show children in cohabiting arrangements fare worse developmentally than their counterparts in other arrangements (Brown 2004). In part, this is because cohabiting unions among low-income families are often short-lived, and children are more likely to move more frequently (Bumpass and Lu 2000). This itinerant existence takes a toll on children's academic achievement (Hanushek, Kain, and Rivkin 2004; Haveman and Wolfe 1995; Ingersoll, Scamman, and Eckerling 1989; McLanahan and Sandefur 1994) and can contribute to behavioral problems (Adam and Chase-Lansdale 2002). Moving frequently also disrupts children's social networks by severing ties with friends, schools, and community institutions (McLanahan and Sandefur 1994).

The ultimate gamble in all this was whether income gains would offset the other trade-offs that the poor must contend with daily. As DeParle asks in *American Dream*, which features the lives of three mothers and their 10 children in the postwelfare world, "How much will low-wage work alone change the trajectory of underclass life? What if the mothers' jobs leave them poor? What if they're still stuck in the ghetto? What if their kids still lack fathers?" (DeParle 2004, p. 113).

SURPRISING RESULTS: CASELOADS PLUMMET

To the surprise of many, welfare caseloads fell quickly and dramatically in the years following the passage of PRWORA. Poverty among single mothers declined from 42 percent in 1996 to 33 percent in 2000 (Jencks 2005). Among their children, the poverty rate fell from 54 percent in 1993 to 43 percent in 2005 (U.S. Census Bureau n.d.). In most states, caseloads were cut in half and have continued to decline, although at a slower pace than in the early years. Between 1996 and 2003, for example, caseloads declined 53 percent in Michigan (the focus of our study here), 57 percent in Wisconsin (the "birthplace" of welfare reform), and 84 percent in Illinois (home to a large, urban city, Chicago) (U.S. Department of Health and Human Services 2007).

The extent to which PRWORA itself was responsible for these caseload declines remains the subject of some debate in the research world. The Council of Economic Advisers (1999), among others, find that welfare reform and other social policy changes at the time contributed, at most, to about one-third of the decline in welfare caseloads. Instead, the economy, which between 1992 and 2000 pumped more than 20 million jobs into the pipeline, was a much bigger player. Another contributing factor was the EITC, which Clinton expanded greatly just prior to reform. The EITC, which provides up to $4,000 in tax refunds to low-wage workers, has been called the single most important antipoverty policy in the decade (Blank 1998, p. 113). The program has been credited with lifting millions out of poverty—4.4 million in 2003 alone, more than one-half of them children. Without the EITC, the poverty rate among children would be 25 percent higher (Holt 2006). In addition, the country's workforce had been shifting steadily away from manufacturing and toward services, with its lower demands for education. For women leaving welfare, many of whom lacked skills and education, the service sector was a place to gain a foothold.

In the aftermath of welfare reform, the race to the bottom never materialized, and many women are indeed working and earning slightly more, on average. The employment rate nationally of low-educated, single-mothers increased from 62 percent in 1996 to 73 percent in 2000 before falling to 69 percent by 2005 after a brief recession (Parrott and

Sherman 2006). In 2008, 71.4 percent of mothers in female-headed households were employed (U.S. Census Bureau 2009).

However, rising rates of employment among less-educated single mothers have not eradicated material hardships. Families experiencing such hardships in the postwelfare world are the most vulnerable, having lost an important source of income when they left welfare. Thus, they may be particularly at risk during periods of unemployment. In fact, it may be these most vulnerable women who have contributed to the rise in *severe* poverty (those with incomes less than 70 percent of the poverty threshold) between 1996 and 2003, even as overall poverty rates declined (Jencks, Winship, and Swingle 2006). That is, although many single mothers have more income today, the poorest among them do not. Jared Bernstein and Mark Greenberg, writing in *American Prospect* in 2001, reported that one-third of those who had left welfare (both working and nonworking mothers) had to cut the size of meals or skip them because there wasn't enough food, 39 percent reported being unable to pay rent in the last year, and 7 percent were forced to move in with others.

THE LOW-WAGE JOB MARKET

It is perhaps not surprising that in the first years following welfare reform, women still struggled to make ends meet. Nationally, wages among those who had left welfare were between $7 and $8 per hour (Acs and Loprest 2004). For a full-time job, these wages translate into roughly $18,000 a year. "Good jobs" are often elusive for former welfare recipients.

The types of jobs these single mothers were finding, in addition to being low-pay, were often unstable, with hours that could change in a minute's notice. Presser and Cox (1997) find that more than 40 percent of all working mothers aged 18–43 who lack postsecondary education—a category into which many welfare recipients fall—work nonstandard schedules (see also Henley and Lambert [2005]). As a 2007 policy paper by the Center for Law and Social Policy outlines, less-educated workers, younger workers, and African Americans are disproportionately working night or evening hours. Only 39 percent of low-wage workers received paid time off, and their "flexible" hours are often flexible only to the employer. Low-wage workers are less likely to be allowed to alter their hours or work from home, and their schedules are often less predictable than workers in higher-paying jobs (Lower-Basch 2007).

Despite these generally low wages and variable work, many argued that welfare reform was a success. Families were working instead of relying on welfare, and because caseloads had declined so precipitously, many states were able to use their block grants to bolster child care subsidies and other work-related supports. But given the generally low wages, unpredictable schedules, and the frequent lack of a spouse or partner to pitch in at home, the question remained, how were these women balancing their work and family responsibilities? Were they, as predicted, sacrificing time with children, both at home and in school? Were they stressed, and was their parenting suffering as a result? Was their mental health on edge? Were their precarious financial situations forcing them to move frequently or double up with other family members or friends? In short, how was the "second shift" in their lives holding up?

MOTHERS' WORK AND CHILDREN'S DEVELOPMENT

As noted above, many scholars and policymakers were particularly concerned about children in families without a safety net and growing work demands on single parents. Poverty is hard on kids, but so too is being stuck in a bad neighborhood with overtaxed schools and overtaxed parents. Yet, evidence from experimental evaluations, in which one group of working families is compared with a control group that is not working and still receiving welfare—considered the gold standard of research—was showing hopeful results for working mothers and their children.

One such evaluation was conducted on the state welfare program in Minnesota, the Minnesota Family Investment Program (MFIP). A distinguishing feature of this program was its added financial incentive to work. A working welfare recipient in Minnesota received a 20 percent boost in her welfare grant to cover work-related expenses, and roughly

40 percent of her earnings were disregarded in calculating the family's grant level. In 1994, a single parent with two children working part time at $6 per hour received $237 more under MFIP than under the old welfare system (Gennetian and Miller 2002). Results from the evaluation show that the MFIP program improved the school performance and reduced behavior problems of young children whose parent was single and a long-term welfare recipient. The gains were significantly greater than those in the control group, whose mothers were not working but still receiving welfare. The key to these positive results was the income supplement the families received in addition to their wages (Gennetian and Miller 2002).

Two other evaluations show more mixed results for children. The Connecticut Jobs First Program was very strict in that a family's entire welfare grant was terminated if the mother reached a 21-month time limit on welfare, but it also allowed working recipients to keep all their earnings up to the federal poverty level as well as their cash assistance for the remainder of the 21 months (Bloom et al. 2002). Jobs First boosted employment and earnings, and it led to small improvements in the behavior of participants' young children. It had mixed effects, however, on the development of adolescent children.

Florida's Family Transition Program limited women to 24 months of welfare in any 60-month period (but with no lifetime limit on welfare use and a wide array of services and incentives to help welfare recipients find work) (Bloom et al. 2000). This program had few impacts, positive or negative, on the well-being of elementary-school-aged children. Among adolescents, however, children whose mothers were working performed somewhat worse than their counterparts in the old AFDC program on a few measures of school performance.

It is not unreasonable to conclude from these evaluations that, on one hand, time limits can be implemented without having widespread severe consequences for families and, on the other, that income supplements in addition to wages of mothers who left welfare may help improve children's development. An important caveat to these findings, however, is that all of the studies were conducted in an unusually strong economic period (1994–2000).

Another notable experiment, New Hope, was conducted in Milwaukee between 1994 and 1998. This program focused on a much broader group than the welfare population, but was also designed to boost income and provide work supports to low-income families. The program is instructive in thinking about what kinds of programs can work for those women who left welfare and joined the ranks of the working poor. New Hope offered low-income workers a wage supplement that averaged $125 per month, health insurance, and a child care subsidy averaging $700 per month, among other supports. As in MFIP, New Hope led to school and behavior improvements among young children five years later. Eight years later, these performance differences would fade while new effects emerged. New Hope children were more engaged in school, and their parents were less likely than control group parents to report that their children had repeated a grade, received poor grades, or been placed in special education. The early results were also stronger for boys. School results such as these are important because doing better in school can increase the likelihood that children will remain engaged and not drop out or seriously falter. For boys in inner-city schools in particular, dropping out is a too-frequent temptation, with the lure of gangs and other trouble right around the corner (Duncan, Huston, and Weisner 2007; Miller et al. 2008).

One caveat to the generally positive findings, however, is outcomes for teens. Whereas a mother's employment improved school performance and behavior for young children, it often had the opposite effect on teenagers. The MFIP evaluation, for example, finds that when parents increase employment, adolescents are at increased risk for school difficulties (Gennetian and Miller 2002). One explanation for the adverse impacts on teenage children is that they are shouldering the burden of caring for younger siblings while their mothers are at work.

Other research (albeit not random assignment experimental studies) lends support to these findings. In these studies, the type of job mattered. In particular, a mother's unstable employment was often associated with greater risk of dropping out of school among teens and increased behavior and mental health issues (Chase-Lansdale et al. 2003; Gennetian, Lopoo, and London 2008; and Kalil and Ziol-Guest 2005). Likewise, work intensity can take a toll on children. Studies also show that full-time work, compared with part-time, increases the likelihood that teens will skip school or act out in class and see their grades decline (Gennetian, Lopoo, and London 2008). Although few have studied the effects on children of parents who work nonstandard hours (night shift or weekends, for example), one can easily imagine that such work schedules can stress parent-child relationships. One study shows that the increased stress posed by nonstandard work hours can increase children's behavior problems and harm school performance (Joshi and Bogen 2007).

The culprit in these poorer outcomes, some have surmised, may be a lack of oversight after school and in the evenings. Consider Debra, whom Katherine Newman and Margaret Chin (2002) profile in an *American Prospect* article. Working the afternoon shift, Debra had to rely on her 10-year-old to care for her younger children, time that should have been reserved for school work and playing with her own friends. Her daughter had already been held back in school once and was still struggling academically. Being called on to care for her young siblings was likely an added responsibility that was detrimental to her academic life. Indeed, in interviews with low-income mothers, a frequent fear was that without proper supervision and monitoring, their children would let homework slide and fall victim to the lure of the neighborhood. As Toni, whom Kristin Seefeldt interviewed in an in-depth qualitative study of participants in the Michigan Women's Employment Study (Seefeldt 2008), said, "My kids are teenagers, and [with] teenagers, I think a parent needs to be at home when they're home because they get carried away . . . I experienced that already with my oldest son, so I don't want to make that same mistake with these two." Other women feared that their teenage daughters would become pregnant if they were not home to keep an eye on them.

In *The Missing Class*, Katherine Newman and Victor Tan Chen (2007) chronicle the lives of several families who are teetering on the brink between working class and poverty. Many of the mothers had used welfare in the past, and were now working hard to escape the clutch of poverty. One mother, Tamar Guerra, was doing everything right, according to welfare reformers. She was working, she was married, and she was earning an above-poverty wage. However, her son Omar was feeling this success differently.

Tamar's job far across town demanded that she leave early in the morning, returning home after 6:00 p.m., when she made dinner and then "passed out in an armchair" from exhaustion. Her absence after school and her exhaustion after dinner left Omar on his own, when before Tamar had been vigilant about making him study. Not surprisingly, Omar's homework was not getting done, and teachers were calling frequently. Tamar's youngest son's grades had also begun to slide. Gradually Omar disengaged from school, cutting classes to do odd jobs in the neighborhood, until at age 15, he embarked on a new, seriously destructive path. He and two other boys were accused of sexually assaulting a young woman, and Omar was sent to a juvenile detention facility in upstate New York for 18 months.

Tamar was fortunate enough to have regular hours. Olivia, an African American mother of three whom Seefeldt (2008) interviewed, worked various shifts at a call center, sometimes a normal 8–5 shift, sometimes 12–9 p.m. The job was stressful—200 workers confined to cubicles fielding calls from often irritated customers under a stop clock. To add to the stress, not being able to depend on a regular schedule disrupted Olivia's sleep, but more important, it did not allow her to spend time with her children. She often worked through dinner and lamented the fact that her children ate hot dogs on those nights. Most recently, her son had been in a fight at school, and the principal had called Olivia to come and get him. Her supervisor refused to let her go, telling her to find someone else to pick up her son.

The uncertain hours, low wages, and often monotonous or highly structured work environments leave women tired and frazzled at the end of a day. Anita, another woman whom Seefeldt (2008) interviewed, talked about how work was interfering with what she saw as a woman's primary job: being a mother. Once, she said, the job of a mother was to take care of the household. Today, Anita's friend with two children has to "do it all," and be the breadwinner too. "She's doing it . . . but it's hurting the kids. One of them, which is my godchild, she can barely read. And it's like, when her mama get home, she's tired. It's hard for her to spend the time, to take the time out." Denise, a 32-year-old woman in Seefeldt's study who managed a trucking company, summed it up for many women working what Arlie Hochschild (1989) has called the "second shift": "It gets stressful, taking care of everything, being both mom and dad and then having to work." Perhaps the most poignant of the comments is from Caroline, who also appears in Seefeldt's book: "There are days," she says, "where you just want to put your head down and you just feel like crying."

THE FOCUS OF THE BOOK

The federal and state policy emphasis on mandated work in exchange for receipt of cash assistance is unlikely to change. Most recently, Congress passed, and President Bush signed into law, legislation that reauthorized the TANF program of 1996. The Deficit Reduction Act of 2005 requires states to engage more TANF cases in productive work activities leading to self-sufficiency (U.S. Department of Health and Human Services n.d.). Single parents are required to participate in work activities for at least 30 hours per week. Two-parent families must participate in work activities between 35 and 55 hours a week, depending on circumstances.

These policies have focused on pushing low-income women into work, in part because policymakers think doing so will benefit children. It is not clear, however, that this will be true when many of the women leaving welfare for work are likely to land jobs that make it difficult to balance work and family.

It is this balance—or lack thereof—and its effects on children that we focus on in this monograph. We pay particular attention to the nature of work. We explore the effects of work that are stable or unstable, the number of hours worked in a week, the regularity of the schedule, and its flexibility, among other things. If we can draw any lessons now from welfare reform, it is that work per se is not a bad thing for single-mother families. In fact, work can bring stability, routine, and a sense of pride to a woman and her family, just as Clinton said. However, peeling back the curtain shows that the type of work, the number of hours worked, and the flexibility of the job—in other words, the nature of the work—is key.

The next chapter provides a description of Michigan's welfare policies followed by a description of the Women's Employment Study. We then present the structure of our analysis—the data, measures, and methods we use to analyze the outcomes—and describe the findings. We conclude with some thoughts on what these findings might mean for future policies in a postwelfare world.

Notes

1. Public Law 100-485. Family Support Act of 1988. October 13, 1988.
2. Clinton had originally campaigned on the bumper-sticker slogan, "Two years and you're off," but reformers softened the message.
3. Many of these ideas were outlined in David Ellwood's book, *Poor Support* (1988). Ellwood's policy prescriptions for reforming welfare and ending poverty included providing universal medical protection, bolstering the earnings of low-wage workers, strengthening the child support system, retaining a welfare safety net for families suffering temporary setbacks, and offering government jobs of last resort.
4. Evidence of just how radically thinking had shifted in a decade, the book was labeled a "thought experiment" in 1984 because no mainstream politician would then touch it.
5. Turner was a member of the Wisconsin group, led by Governor Tommy Thompson, who used Clinton's offer of state control of welfare programs to usher in much stricter requirements, including firm time limits, of welfare recipients than Clinton's plan proposed. Indeed, Wisconsin's model would be a major influence on the final welfare reform bill. Danziger (1997).
6. In a robust economy, more people are able to find work, and caseloads will typically decline. This was evident in the years immediately following passage of PWROWA, when the country was in the midst of a very robust economy. After 2001, however, most states saw increases in their TANF caseloads, in part due to worsening economic conditions.

2
The Women's Employment Study—Context and Content

Welfare and other policies targeted to low-income families were changing fundamentally both nationally and in Michigan as our study got under way. We describe some of the most important changes here before describing our study in detail.

THE POLICY CONTEXT IN MICHIGAN

Prior to the welfare reform legislation of 1996, the federal government allowed states to experiment with different approaches to welfare programs by opting out of the requirements of the old welfare system and developing their own welfare policies. Michigan was at the cutting edge of such experimentation and was the second state to file for such a "waiver" from the federal rules in 1992. By 1996, 27 states had implemented a major welfare waiver of some kind (Schoeni and Blank 2000). Many of the new policies were precursors to the Temporary Assistance for Needy Families (TANF) legislation enacted in 1996: they contained work requirements accompanied by time limits on public assistance and punishments (or sanctions) for those who did not follow the new rules. Because of these early reforms to its state welfare system, Michigan was prepared to act quickly when the federal government enacted welfare reform legislation nationwide in 1996.

State approaches to welfare policies vary dramatically. Michigan's early plan emphasized jobs over education and training (that is, it took a "work first" approach), and the state used a variety of policy tools to both encourage work and punish those who did not comply. Michigan's original TANF plan required recipients to work or participate in approved job search activities for at least 20 hours per week (Seefeldt et al. 1998). The weekly work-hour requirement increased to 25 hours by

1999, 30 hours in 2000, and 40 hours in 2002. Recipients whose youngest child was under age 6 were required to work 20 hours per week.

As a further incentive to work, the state garnished the welfare checks of those mothers who refused to work. "Noncompliers," as they were called, faced a 25 percent reduction in benefits for four months, followed by the complete termination of their benefits if they still refused to follow the new work rules. Recipients who had been receiving assistance for fewer than 60 days faced immediate termination from the welfare rolls if they failed to abide by the work requirements (Seefeldt and Anderson 2000). In addition, local offices could implement even more severe sanction policies at their discretion (Seefeldt et al. 2001). In terms of both the extent of the cut and the sanction's length, Michigan's sanction policies fell in the middle compared with policies being enacted at that time in other states (Urban Institute 2004). At the stricter end, some states' sanction policies imposed more severe cuts in families' grants (for example, 39 states eliminated the grant entirely), and others, such as Pennsylvania, made these cuts permanent.

In another change under Michigan's welfare reform program, women were no longer eligible for cash assistance once their incomes from work pushed them above the income eligibility guidelines, which in 1997 stood at $774 a month. Most women who followed the work requirements described above reached this income limit rather quickly and therefore lost their welfare payments. Some states had much higher income eligibility limits, meaning that more working families would be eligible for welfare (for example, Iowa's ceiling was $1,065 per month), while others were much lower (for example, $402 per month in Texas [State Policy Documentation Project 1999]).

Michigan also implemented an "income disregard" policy that allowed families to keep more of their cash assistance while working (so long as they remained under the income eligibility limits just described). In this regard as well, Michigan fell somewhere in the middle compared with other states. In Michigan, recipients were able to disregard the first $200 of their monthly earnings as well as 20 percent of the rest of their monthly income when determining eligibility for assistance (State Policy Documentation Project 1999). This policy made work more attractive than before because it allowed women to combine welfare and work up until the point at which they reached the income limit noted above. Some states, such as Indiana and Missouri, maintained the more restrictive prewelfare reform limits, which made it almost impossible to work at all and remain eligible for welfare. Others, such as Kentucky and Connecticut, allowed women to keep all their earnings for a period of time while remaining eligible for welfare (Crouse 1999).

In other regards, Michigan's welfare policies were more generous than most other states: the maximum monthly benefit in 2000 was $459 for a family of three compared with a median monthly benefit of $415 in the United States as a whole (Crouse 1999). However, Michigan's monthly benefit level has not risen since 1993, meaning that its real value has declined over time. Michigan also made funding for child care more accessible than did most other states, offering subsidies to all families with children under age 13 with an income less than 188 percent of the federal poverty line (or $26,064 per year for a family of three in 1999), regardless of whether they were receiving welfare. In addition, anyone receiving welfare was categorically eligible for child care assistance. As of 2001, Michigan had no waiting list for child care grants, meaning all eligible families could receive assistance. However, research suggests that most eligible families in Michigan did not apply for child care assistance (Seefeldt et al. 2001).

Finally, unlike most other states, Michigan did not impose a time limit on the receipt of public assistance. Rather, the state planned to use state funds to provide assistance to individuals reaching the lifetime welfare receipt limit of five years that was mandated by the federal government (Urban Institute 2004). Michigan was among only a handful of states that allowed families to continue benefits after the federally mandated 60-month period, making the state more generous than most others in time limit policies. In comparison, 24 states imposed a 60-month limit on welfare benefits and completely terminated families' benefits after the 60-month period, while 19 states had time limits less than 60 months (Zedlewski, Holcomb, and Loprest 2007).

During the period covered by our study, Michigan's publicly provided health insurance was also relatively generous. In 1997, Michigan provided health insurance to all children aged 6–18 whose family incomes were below 150 percent of the federal poverty line (a total household income of $19,396 for a single mother with two children); starting in 1998 eligibility expanded to all children with incomes below

200 percent of the poverty line ($26,266 per year), which stretched well beyond what the federal government required states to provide. Only 14 states were more generous in their coverage of school-aged children (National Governors Association 2003).

As a whole, these policies created both opportunities and constraints for welfare leavers in Michigan. On the one hand, welfare became much less attractive because women were required to work or prepare and search for work. The emphasis on work increased over time, as the minimum hourly work requirement for welfare recipients increased steadily. Recipients not meeting these requirements faced strict sanctions. Even those following the requirements quickly found that they earned too much money to qualify for welfare.

On the other hand, Michigan instituted several policies designed to make it financially feasible for women to go to work, including child care subsidies, earnings disregards, no time limits on welfare receipt, and generous health insurance benefits. Finally, and importantly, the economy was very strong in the years immediately following reform in 1996, making it relatively easy for women to find jobs at the beginning of the study. Unemployment rates in Michigan bottomed out at 3.7 percent in 2000, although they would then rise during the economic slowdown at the turn of the century to 7.1 percent in 2003. Unemployment rates for the county in which the Women's Employment Study (WES) took place followed the same pattern, but were on average one to two percentage points higher, reflecting its position as a relatively more economically disadvantaged county in the state.

THE DATA SOURCE: WOMEN'S EMPLOYMENT STUDY

We now turn to a fuller description of our data. The data used in this analysis come from the Women's Employment Study (WES), which was a survey of 753 low-income single mothers in Michigan who were interviewed five times between 1997 and 2003. The WES was conducted at the University of Michigan's Poverty Research and Training Center (now the National Poverty Center). This sample of mothers came from the welfare rolls in one urban Michigan county; specifically, the sample was randomly drawn from a list of single mothers in that county who were receiving welfare in February 1997, were either white or African American, and were between the ages of 18 and 54. This sample excludes mothers who were not receiving welfare in February 1997. It is possible that welfare reform policies had the effect of discouraging women from applying for welfare, or restricting the number or type of women who were able to receive welfare in the first place. If so, then such dynamics are missed in our analysis.

Of 874 women selected to take part in the study, 86 percent, or 753, agreed to participate (Danziger et al. 2000). Researchers completed the first wave of WES interviews between August and December 1997. Among the 753 mothers interviewed, researchers selected 575 who had a child between the ages of 2 and 10 to take part in a special study focused on their children's well-being. These families made up the "target child sample," and researchers asked mothers additional questions assessing parenting and child well-being in each survey. The analyses presented in this monograph use data from questions asked about these target children.

Researchers collected a second wave of data in 1998, a third wave in late 1999, a fourth wave in early 2002, and a fifth and final wave in 2003. No other welfare reform study has followed a panel of respondents for this length of time, making the WES an important data set for examining the life experiences of welfare leavers. By the fifth wave, 378 children remained who were in the original target child sample (66 percent of the original sample). Researchers have found no differences in race, age, education, earnings, or the number of people in the household between women who dropped out of the survey and those who stayed until the final wave of data collection (Cadena and Pape 2006). However, those women remaining in the study were more likely to continue to receive welfare over time compared with the participants who dropped out of the study.

We now turn to a description of how we measure children's behavior and mothers' employment patterns.

MEASURES

Outcome Measures

We use several measures of child adjustment as dependent variables in our analysis (i.e., the key "outcome measures" that we think may be influenced by a mother's employment). The first three measures are *externalizing behavior problems*, *internalizing behavior problems*, and the *total behavior problems* scales. Mothers answered a series of questions designed to gauge her child's behavior. These questions have been developed, tested by others, and judged as valid measures in that they are related to other important dimensions of children's well-being, such as test scores. The items come from the Behavioral Problems Index (BPI), a widely used measure of children's behavior (Chase-Lansdale et al. 1991). Due to space constraints, the WES used a subset of items from the BPI at each wave of data collection. However, the full set of items was collected in the final wave, and we make use of this fuller set of questions in our longer-run analyses.

Externalizing behavior (consisting of three items) includes questions such as whether the child "bullies or is cruel or mean to others" or "breaks things deliberately." Mothers respond whether these behaviors are not true, sometimes true, or often true for their child. The lowest score possible on this measure is 3, where a mother reports that none of the behaviors are true for her child. The highest score possible is a 9, where a mother says that each of the three behaviors is often true of her child.

The five questions in the *internalizing behavior* scale ask mothers about things such as whether her child is unhappy or sad, withdrawn, or feels worthless. The highest score possible on this scale is 15, which would represent a mother who says each of the five behaviors is often true for her child. The lowest possible score is 5, a report that none of the behaviors ever applies to her child.

Our measure of *total behavior problems* is a 12-item summary index that combines the externalizing and internalizing subscales and includes four additional items measuring fear and anxiety in the child that were consistently reported for waves 2 though 5. Thus, for each of these measures, a higher score reflects greater behavior problems.

The other child outcomes we examine are school-related measures based on maternal reports of whether the child had exhibited *disruptive and/or disobedient behavior problems in school* (defined as sometimes or often displaying such behavior), whether the child had been *placed in special education* since the last interview, whether the child had *repeated a grade* since the last time the mother was interviewed, and whether the child had experienced *school absenteeism problems* (defined as regularly missing school at least one or more times a month during the time since the last interview). These variables have a score of 1 if the event occurred and 0 otherwise.

All measures of child well-being are based on mothers' reports. Relying solely on mothers to gauge their children's well-being can be problematic for several reasons. First, mothers who are doing well may report that their children are doing well, and mothers who are having a hard time may do the opposite. Therefore, the measures of children's behavior and experiences may not accurately reflect how the child is doing, but rather how the mother is doing at a given point in time. Our use of standard econometric approaches (called fixed-effects regression), described below, can help to address this issue by controlling for stable (i.e., unchanging with time) characteristics of mothers, such as her sense of well-being.

Another potential problem is that mothers may not be good reporters of how their children are doing, and their reports may not capture their children's actual functioning. Mothers may not directly observe their children's behavior (for example, in school), or they may not be attuned to it. Other researchers have attempted to examine the extent of these issues when using maternal reports. In one study, researchers asked mothers the same behavior problems questions two weeks apart and examined whether their reports changed over time. Results indicated that although mothers changed their reports on individual items measuring children's behavior over the two-week period, when these items were combined in a scale, the overall measure of children's behavior was quite stable, with over 60 percent of the scores remaining the same over the two-week period. This suggests that mothers are, on the whole, not changing their reports of children's behavior in response to transitory changes in their own lives. Other researchers have documented that the Behavior Problems Index is associated with other, more clearly observed aspects of children's well-being. For example, children with poorer behavior also have lower test scores. This suggests that, despite the problems of using mother-reported data, these reports of children's behavior are generally stable over time, and do capture how well children are doing (Center for Human Resource Research 1993).

Characterizing Maternal Employment Patterns

To predict these measures of children's well-being, we focus on several important aspects of mothers' employment. First, we include in our analysis a measure of whether a mother worked at all between waves of data collection. Nearly 90 percent of mothers did so. The diversity in work involvement among our sample lies not in whether mothers worked, but in the significant variation in the nature and pattern of that employment (e.g., job quality, job stability versus instability, and upward mobility versus employment in dead-end jobs), the number and regularity of hours worked, and flexibility of work schedule. As a result, the work versus nonworking comparison is less useful than is identifying differential effects in the type of maternal work involvement on child well-being.

Including an indicator of whether a mother worked allows our analysis to control for, or hold constant, whether a mother was working or not and to ask the following question: "When mothers work, how do conditions of her job, such as its stability or the predictability of its work hours, influence children's development?" If we did not control for whether a mother was working, it would be difficult to know what our measure of "fluctuating hours," for example, was capturing; the effect on children of working fluctuating hours compared with nonwork (which is not our primary interest), or the effect of fluctuating hours compared with work at predictable hours (which is our primary interest).

The second key measure reflects mothers' *job transitions* between waves of data collection. We characterize employment patterns and the extent of job stability and job mobility between waves, using mothers' reports gathered at each wave on job tenure, monthly job/employment history, and reported reason for job separation (if any occurred). This measure includes information on whether any job changes resulted from involuntary job separations, as well as job changes that were initiated by women due to child care concerns and/or concerns about their children's health.[1] We can distinguish job transitions as voluntary or involuntary (i.e., due to being laid off or fired), and whether they were followed by a nonemployment spell of four or more weeks.

In our main analyses, we examine three patterns of job transitions: *job stability, job mobility,* and *job instability*. Individuals whose current or most recent job at a given wave was the same as that held at the previous wave have *job stability* (this is the group to which all others are compared in our analysis). *Job mobility* occurs when a respondent makes a voluntary job change from one wave to the next, without experiencing any involuntary separations or transitions into nonwork, and the interval between jobs is less than four weeks. Conversely, we define *job instability* as being laid off or fired. Also included in this category are women who quit a job because of dissatisfaction with their current jobs, for reasons such as inadequate pay, poor working conditions, suboptimal hours, poor job match, or transportation problems, with an intervening spell of nonemployment of at least one month. This definition has been used by other researchers as well (Gladden and Taber 2000; Royalty 1998). Job changes that are driven by maternal concerns for child care or the general well-being of the child are not considered in our measure of job instability; they are classified as voluntary job mobility.[2]

Our main analyses also include a variable indicating whether the mother *worked full time*, defined as 35 or more hours per week in the current or most recent job as of the survey date. We also include a variable measuring whether the mother reported that her job entailed *fluctuating work hours*, derived from a question asking, "Does the number of hours you work from week to week change a lot, a fair amount, a little, or hardly at all?" and identifying mothers who answered "a lot" or "a fair amount."

In some analyses, we use a measure of job quality based on the wage, health benefits, and hours of a woman's primary job that is quite similar to the notions embodied in living wage laws. We define a "good" job as one that is full time (at least 35 hours per week), pays at least $7 per hour, and offers health benefits either immediately or after a trial period, or, as one that is full time, pays at least $8.50 per hour, and does not provide health benefits.[3] Individuals whose current jobs satisfy these wage and benefit criteria but who work part time are defined as having a good job if they are working part time voluntarily. All other jobs are defined as "bad" jobs (as defined by Johnson and Corcoran [2003]). At $7 per hour with employer-provided health benefits, the net annual income of a full-time worker is $15,997, 19 percent above the 1999 poverty line for a family of three. At $8.50 per hour without employer-provided health benefits, the net income is $15,212, 13 percent above the 1999 poverty line.

Finally, for our longer-run analyses, we also classify mothers by the work pattern profile experienced over the 1997–2003 study period, defined along the dimensions of job quality, employment stability, and the regularity of work hours described above. For this purpose, we define three different representative work experience profiles that characterize the range of work pattern trajectories among our sample of women. Specifically, *low profile* is defined as not employed in a good job by wave 5 and having experienced chronic job instability and/or fluctuating work hours for the vast majority of the study period (i.e., either she had been fired or laid off two or more times, had experienced four or more voluntary job-to-nonemployment transitions, and/or had two or more years of fluctuating work hours over the seven-year study period). Conversely, *high profile* is defined as employed in a good job by wave 5 and had experienced employment stability and regular work hours for the vast majority of the study period (i.e., had not been fired/laid off, had experienced three or fewer voluntary job-to-nonemployment transitions, and had one or fewer periods of fluctuating work hours over the seven-year study period). *Medium profile* is defined as not employed in good job by wave 5, some job instability or fluctuating work hours, but not persistently so to be categorized as *low profile*, nor was improvement in work trajectory great enough to be categorized as *high profile*. We use these three maternal work experience profiles to predict child outcomes at the end of the study.

As with the measure of children's outcomes, our measures of maternal employment experiences are also based on mothers' self-reports. Mothers are also reporting on employment experiences that occurred over a period of one to two years. The survey data on work hours, earnings, and retrospective event-history reports of employment were collected in the same fashion as collected in nationally representative longitudinal surveys such as the Panel Study of Income Dynamics.[4]

Other Controls

Because many other factors besides maternal employment can also influence child behavior, it is important to measure and account for as many of these factors as possible. This allows us to test the independent effect of each measure of maternal employment on child behavior. In this study, we wanted to control for factors that might influence children's well-being but would not themselves be influenced by mothers' employment (these are often referred to as exogenous measures). Therefore, our analyses control for (that is, hold constant) the following measures: child age, race (whether African American or white), and gender. We also control for the mother's age and education, the latter using the following measures: whether the mother dropped out of high school, whether she completed high school but had no other years of schooling, or whether she attended college. In addition, we include an index capturing the home literacy environment from the total of four items asking if anyone in the household 1) has a library card, 2) uses the library card, 3) subscribes to newspapers or magazines, and 4) whether the respondent ever reads to herself.[5]

We also control for mothers' living arrangements, using measures indicating whether she was married, cohabiting with romantic partner, or single, and whether the child's grandmother lives in the household. We also include a measure of father involvement in childrearing using a scale composed of four mother-reported items (each item ranges from 1 to 4, where higher numbers indicate greater involvement). The four questions are 1) how often the target child sees his or her biological father; 2) how often the respondent and the biological father discuss the target child; 3) how well the respondent and the target child get along; and 4) how often the biological father provides diapers, clothing, or other items. Because family structure and living arrangements influence child development outcomes, we control for these measures in our main models so that we do not mistakenly attribute their influences to those of maternal employment patterns.[6]

SNAPSHOT OF THE STUDY PARTICIPANTS

Before moving on, it is useful to provide a snapshot of the women and children in our study. This information is presented in Table 2.1, which presents averages for all of the measures used in our analyses.

Demographic Characteristics of Mothers and Their Living Arrangements

At the beginning of our study, mothers in our sample were, on average, 30 years old (Table 2.1). A little more than one-half (56 percent) of respondents were African American and 44 percent were white. About 28 percent of mothers did not complete high school, while 38 percent completed no other education beyond high school. In terms of the family living arrangements of children in the WES, 12 percent of women were married and 19 percent were cohabiting (that is, living with a romantic partner in the household), on average, across the entire study period. For the most part, though, these partners were not the biological fathers of the WES focal children, as only 7 percent of children lived with their biological father in the household. Despite this, measures of father involvement were relatively high, reaching almost 10 points on a scale of 4–16 (as measured at wave 1). Mothers in the WES were more likely to live with their own mothers (the child's grandmother) than with a spouse; 19 percent of women lived in such a three-generational arrangement at the first wave and 14 percent, on average, across all waves. The home literacy environment was quite high (with an average of 3.15 out of a possible 4 points total).

Characteristics of the Children

At the first interview in 1997, the average age of the target children was 4.7 years. Pooling across all waves, the average age of the children was 7 (Table 2.1). By 2003, at the fifth interview, the children were between the ages of 5 and 17, with an average age of 10.75 years. The children in this sample, on average, display significantly more externalizing behavior problems than the average U.S. child, including behavior such as acting out, bullying others, or breaking things. In the

Table 2.1 Descriptive Statistics of WES Mothers and Children, 1997–2003

Mothers' characteristics	
Maternal age (years)	29.7
White (%)	44.0
Black (%)	56.0
High school dropout (%)	27.5
High school $grad_t$ (%)	37.9
Some $college_t$ (%)	34.6
Married (%)	12.0
Cohabitating (%)	18.7
Single (%)	66.3
Grandmother resides in household (%)	13.5
Child's biological father in household (%)	7.1
Father involvement $index_{WI}$ (range 4–16)	9.67
Home literacy environment $index_{WI}$ (range 0–4)	3.15
Child characteristics	
Boy (%)	49.5
Girl (%)	50.5
Child age (years)	6.7
Child outcomes	
Externalizing behavior	4.69
Internalizing behavior problem index	6.05
Total behavior problem index	16.9
Incidence of involvement in school-related problems	
Disruptive problems in $school_t$ (%)	34.2
School absenteeism $problem_t$ (%)	19.6
Ever throughout survey (%)	
Disruptive problems in school	67.7
School absenteeism problem	47.2
Repeated a grade	26.4
Placed in special ed.	19.7
Repeated a grade or placed in special ed.	36.8

WES, mothers' reports of their children's externalizing behavior problems were higher (rating a score of 4.69) compared with a score of 3.95 in the 1997 Panel Study of Income Dynamics Child Development Supplement, which is representative of all children aged 2–12 in the United States. However, children in the WES had similar levels of internalizing behavior problems as those in that same national sample (6.05 vs. 5.96 [authors' calculations]).

We also find frequent school-related behavior problems. On average found across the waves, about 34 percent of the WES children between ages 5 and 15 were disruptive in school, and 20 percent had missed school at least one or more times per month. Although we lack data to adequately compare these findings nationally, they appear quite high. Furthermore, these children quite frequently repeat a grade or are placed into special education. By the end of the study, roughly one-fourth had repeated a grade, one-fifth had been placed in special education, two-thirds had exhibited disruptive behavior problems in school, and nearly one-half had missed school at least one or more times per month at one of the survey waves over the seven years of the study.

In analyses not shown, we examine the extent and nature of changes in children's behavior over time. We find that there is both significant variation across children in their initial levels of behavioral problems as well as in the growth rate of these problem behaviors over time. Although the average single year-to-year change in most behavioral outcomes was small relative to the overall levels of these outcomes, changes in behavior can accumulate and become more substantial problems over the longer run.[7] Substantial minorities of children also experienced changes in being disruptive in school (with 31 percent experiencing a change) and being absent from school at least one or more times per month (23 percent experiencing a change) over the study period. Thus, it appears that WES children's behavior does change over time. Understanding the sources of within- and between-child variation in their adjustment over time is important, and in our later analyses we will attempt to link changes in maternal employment experiences to such changes in behavior.

Work Histories and Financial Situations of Mothers

We next present some characteristics of women in the WES, including some that we do not include in our analyses, in order to give a richer picture of the families we study. By the first interview in the fall of 1997, 23 percent of the women in the WES had left welfare and were working, which increased to 64 percent by 2003.[8] Not surprisingly given the policy changes outlined above, the welfare rolls declined steadily, such that by 2003, fewer than one in five were still receiving welfare. Recall that women continued to receive welfare for as long as they held a job and their incomes did not exceed $774 per month. Finally, a small portion were neither working nor receiving welfare. In 1997, 5 percent fit this description, rising to 18 percent in 2003 (Michigan Program on Poverty and Social Welfare Policy 2004). See Figure 2.1 for more detail.

Over time, the financial situation for women in our sample improved. In 1997, just over one-half (56 percent) lived in households

Figure 2.1 Work and Welfare Status among Women in the WES

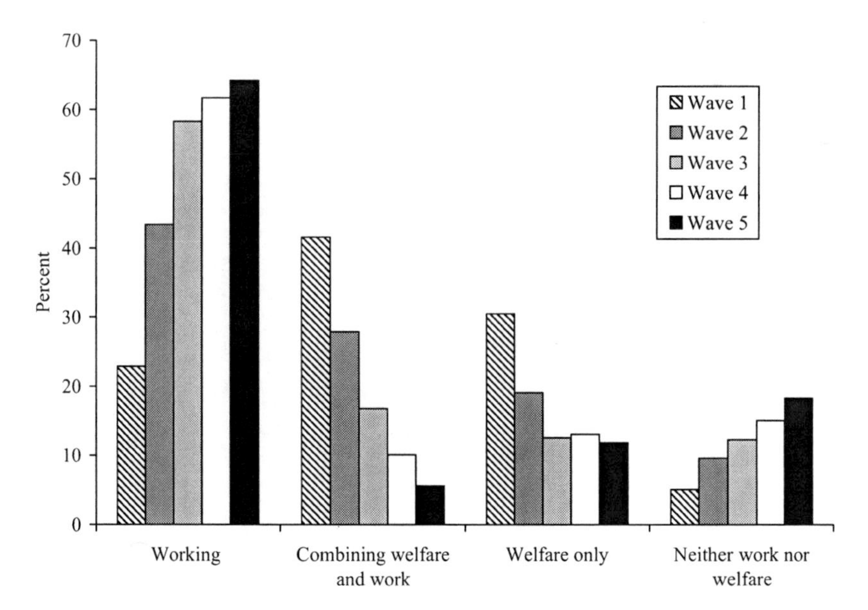

SOURCE: Danziger et al. (2000).

with incomes below the poverty line (annual household income of less than $12,931 for a single mother with two children). By 2003, this had declined to 42 percent (see Figure 2.2). Those who had left welfare for work were doing better financially than the other women in the study, even though as their incomes rose, their public assistance use declined. Clearly, for women in Michigan, it paid to work. That said, wages remained stubbornly low, increasing from $6.74 to $8.15 during the study.

Table 2.2 reports women's employment status at each wave and the wages, hours worked, and job characteristics of working respondents at each wave. The increases in wages, work hours, and health benefits led to improvements in job quality over the study period. At wave 1, only 13.5 percent of working respondents had good jobs; by wave 5, 47 percent of working respondents held good jobs.

The percentage of mothers working full time (at least 35 hours per week) increased steadily, from 45.6 percent in 1997 to 67.7 percent in 2001, but then fell back to 64.9 percent in 2003 (see Table 2.2). However, these overall measures of accumulated work experience mask

Figure 2.2 Percent in Poverty among Women in the WES

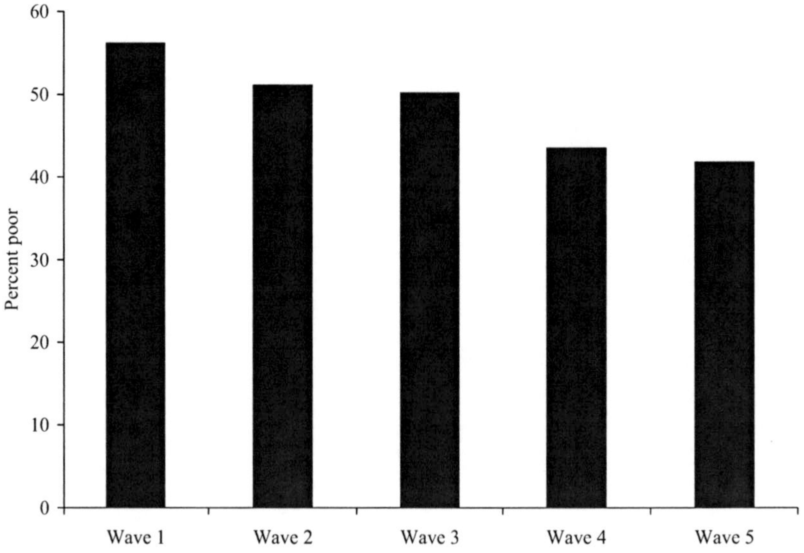

Percent poor

60
50
40
30
20
10
0

Wave 1 Wave 2 Wave 3 Wave 4 Wave 5

SOURCE: Danziger et al. (2000).

significant variation in job skills that have implications for wage growth and job turnover propensities (Johnson 2006). For example, only about 17 percent of women worked in jobs that required reading/writing and computer skills on a daily basis.

Although most of the respondents in our study had worked (much of it full time) in most of the months during the study, job instability was common, as shown in Table 2.3. Pooling across all waves, on average roughly one-half of the respondents experienced job instability from one wave to the next (as defined above), while 29.6 percent experienced job stability, and 21.9 percent moved to jobs with better pay or working conditions without intervening spells of nonemployment. The most common reason for changing jobs was being laid off or fired. About one-fourth of women who changed jobs between waves did so for this reason, and, looking over the entire study period, 35 percent of women were fired or laid off at some point.[9]

We asked women who were working at wave 1 if they expected to be working in their current jobs less than six months, six months to one year, one to two years, or more than two years. Sixty-three percent of those working at wave 1 expected to be working in the same job at wave 2, but in reality only 38 percent did. Nevertheless, the fraction of women who experienced job stability over a two-year period more than doubled from fall 1999 to fall 2001, relative to the fraction of women who experienced job stability during the preceding two-year period (increasing from 12.5 percent to 33.1 percent [data not shown]).

On the other hand, the worsening economic conditions in 2001 increased the risk of job loss. Among individuals who experienced job separations between waves, separations resulting from being fired or laid off increased from 21.3 percent to 27.9 percent between 1998–1999 and 1999–2001. As the economy contracts, individuals with the weakest skills and least work experience lose their jobs first, leaving many former or current recipients highly vulnerable to layoffs. Prior work has documented that the business cycle downturn in 2001 had significant negative impacts on the job quality and job transition patterns of former/current recipients (Johnson and Corcoran 2003).

Roughly one-quarter of the women in our sample fit the low-profile work trajectory definition over the study period characterized by chronic instability. On the other end of the spectrum, an equal-sized proportion

Table 2.2 Summary Statistics of Maternal Work Involvement, WES 1997–2003

						Percentage-point change between		
Labor market status[a] and employment characteristics	Wave 1 Fall 1997	Wave 2 Fall 1998	Wave 3 Fall 1999	Wave 4 Fall 2001	Wave 5 Fall 2003	Fall 97–99	Fall 99–01	Fall 97–03
Out of the labor force (%)	10.4	13.3	13.6	9.2	13.1	+3.2 pts	−4.4 pts	+2.7 pts
Unemployed (%)	27.9	21.8	19.6	27.4	23.7	−8.3 pts	+7.8 pts	−4.2 pts
Employed (%)	61.8	64.9	66.8	63.4	63.2	+5.0 pts	−3.4 pts	+1.4 pts
Real hourly wages (expressed in 1999$)								
Mean	6.83	7.20	7.31	8.25	8.28	+7.0%	+12.9%	+26.0%
Median	5.99	6.49	6.94	7.52	7.54	+15.9%	+8.4%	+30.9%
Full time[b] (%)	45.6	59.6	64.9	67.7	64.9	+19.3 pts	+2.8 pts	+19.3 pts
Part time (%)	54.5	40.4	35.2	32.3	35.1	−19.3 pts	−2.8 pts	−19.3 pts
Voluntarily part time (%)	—	13.6	13.6	12.9	13.6	—	−0.7 pts	—
Underemployed[c] (%)	—	26.8	21.6	19.5	21.5	—	−2.1 pts	—
Fluctuating work hours (%)	28.8	22.8	20.6	21.0	17.8	−8.2 pts	+0.4 pts	−11.0 pts
Working in jobs offering health benefits (at any wage) (%)	38.1	54.4	57.1	62.8	56.0	+19.0 pts	+5.7 pts	+17.9 pts
Working full time earning ≥$7/hr (%)	15.1	29.5	37.8	46.3	47.7	+22.7 pts	+8.5 pts	+34.0 pts
Working in bad jobs[d] (%)	86.5	71.2	61.9	54.2	53.0	−24.6 pts	−7.7 pts	−33.5 pts
Working in good jobs (%)	13.5	28.8	38.1	45.8	47.0	+24.6 pts	+7.7 pts	+33.5 pts

NOTE: Numbers in columns 1–5 correspond with waves 1–5 respondents, respectively.

[a] Labor force participants are classified here as individuals who are either currently employed (i.e., at the time of the interview for the relevant wave), or if not employed, have either worked or searched for work within the last year.

[b] Full-time workers are classified here as individuals working at least 35 hours/week on their primary job.

[c] Underemployed workers refer to individuals who work part-time on their primary job, but desire to work more hours on the job. The Wave 1 survey did not contain questions about desired work hours.

[d] We define a "good" job as one that is full-time (at least 35 hours per week), pays at least $7 per hour, and offers health benefits either immediately or after a trial period, or, as one that is full-time, pays at least $8.50 per hour, and does not provide health benefits. Individuals whose current jobs satisfy these wage and benefit criteria but who work part-time are defined as having a good job if they are working part-time voluntarily. All other jobs are defined as "bad" jobs.

Table 2.3 Summary Statistics of Maternal Job Transition Patterns

Average job transition pattern between most recent job of successive waves (%)	
Job stability	30.6
Voluntary job mobility	22.2
Job instability	47.2
Ever fired/laid off $_{(W1\text{–}W5)}$	34.5

fit the high-profile work trajectory characterized by upward mobility with employment stability and regular work hours for the vast majority of the period, and the remaining one-half of women were somewhere in between these two experiences.

Financial hardship was also not unknown. Despite the increases in work participation, many mothers continued to experience economic stress over time, even though family incomes were also rising. Gross monthly income increased by about 50 percent from the beginning to the end of the study period. On average, family gross income was $1,555 per month. Yet, at least one-fifth of the sample reported feeling financially strained at any given survey wave, and about 40–50 percent of mothers reported having been hassled by bill collectors at any one wave. About 22 percent of families, on average over the period, were food insufficient (that is, they sometimes or often did not have enough food in the household), and about one-third of mothers reported receiving food, clothing, or financial assistance from food pantries or churches at any given wave. More than three-quarters of the sample moved at some point across all survey waves. Many of these movers represented transitions to home ownership, but a substantial number of mothers (25 percent) were evicted at some point.

The most common type of job held by women in the WES was a job in the service industry. In 1997, 42 percent of women who were employed worked in the service industry; by 2003 this increased to 50 percent. While some had employment in sales and clerical jobs, the women worked disproportionately in service jobs concentrated in food services (e.g., waitresses or cooks), health services (e.g., nursing aides), cleaning services (e.g., maids or janitors), and personal services (e.g., barber and beauty shops).

Mothers' Health and Mental Health

A striking proportion of women in our sample struggled with physical and mental health issues. A full two-thirds of WES women met diagnostic screening criteria for at least one of six disorders studied (depression, posttraumatic stress, generalized anxiety, social phobia, alcohol dependence, or drug dependence) as defined in the American Psychiatric Association's Diagnostic and Statistical Manual (DSM-V) at some point over the study period.[10] The most common disorder was depression; one-half of the women were clinically depressed at some point during the study. Posttraumatic stress disorder (PTSD) was also quite common, with 40 percent of women meeting the criteria for this disorder at some point over the period of the study. Fewer than 10 percent of the women met the criteria for drug or alcohol dependence.

These rates are substantially higher than national averages for mental health issues. For example, at the first interview, 25 percent of WES women met the criteria for major depressive disorder and 7 percent met the criteria for generalized anxiety disorder; among a national sample of women in 1994, only 13 percent and 4 percent did so, respectively. Similarly, at wave 1, 29 percent of women in the WES were classified as experiencing PTSD at some point over their lifetimes compared with only 10 percent of a national sample of women. Women in the WES were slightly *less* likely than a national sample of women to be classified as having alcohol dependence, but slightly more likely to be classified as having drug dependence (Danziger et al. 2000) (see Figure 2.3).

Health-related issues were also quite common among women in the study. In 2003, one-quarter of the women had a health problem that limited their activities, and 15 percent had a child with a health problem. Strikingly, nearly 40 percent of women reported domestic violence during at least one interview, much higher than the prevalence of domestic violence nationally. For example, at the first interview, 15 percent of WES women reported they were currently experiencing domestic violence, compared to 3 percent of a national sample (Danziger et al. 2000).

Figure 2.3 Comparison between WES and National Samples (12-month prevalence except where noted)

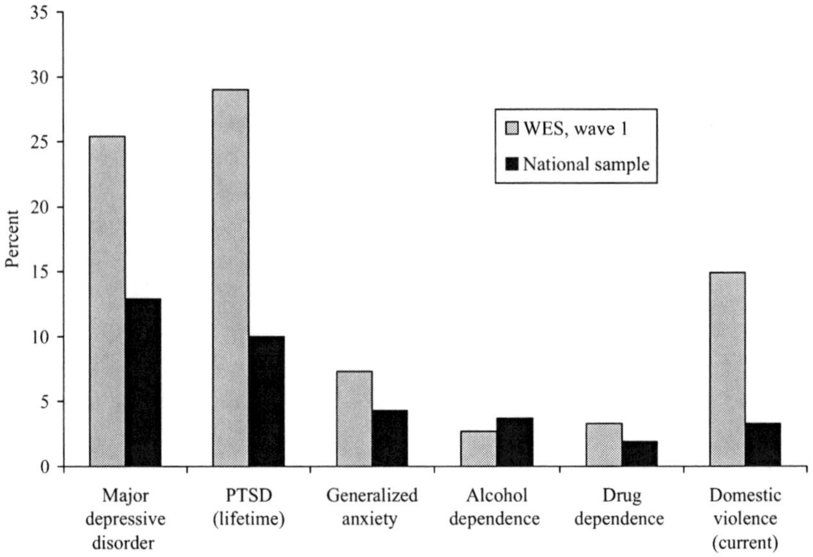

SOURCE: Danziger et al. (2000).

Mothers' Barriers to Work

Many low-income women with welfare histories suffer from a lack of "human capital." They have little education, lack work experience or job skills, and face other barriers to working. Our sample was no different. Among 14 potential barriers to work, 85 percent of the women had at least one barrier, and many had multiple barriers. Past research on this sample showed that low education and little work experience or skills, as well as poor health, drug or alcohol dependence, a lack of transportation, and perceived discrimination were associated with lower likelihoods of working (Danziger et al. 2000).

Relatively few mothers (23 percent) used paid child care for any child, on average across waves. Among the mothers who did use paid child care, however, child care expenditures increased significantly as their work involvement increased over the study period (e.g., monthly child care expenditures increased from $293 at wave 2 to $393 at wave 5; data not shown).

In Short: Precarious Jobs, Precarious Finances and Family Conditions

In summary, a defining characteristic of our sample is that while most women obtained jobs and saw subsequent increases in household income and wages, many women's employment experiences were unstable. Combined with the loss of the stable safety net of welfare assistance, the end result was that the perceived financial situation of these mothers, represented by financial stress, difficulty paying bills, or difficulty obtaining enough food, changed little over time and often remained quite dire. Moreover, for some mothers, work-related expenditures, such as child care, also increased over the study period, thus dampening the income benefits that employment provided. Many of these women also experienced persistent residential instability. These elements of financial stress remained a daily feature of women's lives despite their increasing work participation over time, even though previous analyses have established that women in the WES sample who left welfare for work, or combined welfare and work, were economically better off than their counterparts who remained on welfare and did not work (Danziger et al. 2002). In addition, the levels of children's behavioral adjustment are, in some cases, worse than national averages, suggesting that these children may be at risk.

Thus, the WES consists of a unique sample of women, followed over five waves spanning nearly seven years, during which many were moving off of welfare and into employment. During this time, many women obtained jobs and saw their earnings increase. However, many still suffered from financial hardships, mental health issues, and lack of education and skills. In addition, women's success in leaving welfare for employment varied widely. While some women were able to obtain stable jobs, many others lost jobs or worked unpredictable hours or long days. Key to this study is how these differing work conditions affected the well-being of their children.

THE CONNECTION BETWEEN MOTHERS' EMPLOYMENT AND CHANGES IN CHILD DEVELOPMENT

Child development is a complex process influenced by many factors, only one of which is maternal employment. Child development is also dynamic; children's behavior is influenced by behavior in the past and other past experiences at home, school, in the neighborhood, or elsewhere. To account for such complexities, we need data that follow children over time; that is, we need longitudinal data like the WES.

We believe that a child's past and current experiences combine with the child's innate ability to influence development. This process is shown in Equation (B.1) in Appendix B. We suggest that a child's behavior at a given point is determined by the quality and quantity of time a mother spends with her child up until that point; the quality and quantity of other experiences that the child has had, such as in child care or in school; financial and other investments in children, such as medical care, books, or developmentally appropriate toys; and other characteristics of the child, his or her mother and family, such as family structure (who else is living in the household and the extent of father involvement in child rearing), maternal characteristics such as education, ability or health, and factors such as the child's age, gender, or race.

It is likely that maternal employment could directly influence some of these factors that we believe also play a key role in determining how well a child is doing. For example, when mothers go to work, they may have less time to spend with their children, which may be detrimental for them.[11] However, if going to work increases mothers' self-esteem, financial stability, or mental well-being, then the quality of time that mothers spend with their child may improve, even if the overall quantity declines. Thus, both the quantity and the quality of time a mother spends with her children may be influenced by her work patterns.

In addition, when mothers work, their household income usually increases. As noted above, this was indeed the case with women in the WES. This means that working mothers may have more opportunities to invest in their children by purchasing educational materials, sending their children to enriching programs, or other endeavors. Thus, there are many ways a mother's employment could alter how she invests in her children, and ultimately lead to changes in child well-being.

EMPIRICAL STRATEGY

One difficulty in measuring the effect of maternal employment on children has to do with the issue of choice: the decision to work or stay at home (or the choice of the type of work and number of work hours more generally) may itself be caused by the very child outcomes we wish to examine. For example, a mother whose child acts out may choose a job with more flexible or limited work hours in order to spend more time with that child. This phenomenon is called *reverse causality*. Not accounting for reverse causality can bias the results of a study.

Another issue that complicates analyses occurs when characteristics of mothers that are not evident or that cannot be measured determine both her employment experiences and how well her child is doing. For example, a mother who is highly motivated may hold a stable, flexible job and may have a child who is doing well in school. It would be a mistake, however, to conclude that it is her job that is leading her child to do well in school. Rather, her motivation may be responsible for both the type of job she has and how well her child is doing. This problem is one of *selection bias*. If we do not take account of these issues, our results will be biased and ultimately misleading.

The best way to determine the true influence of mothers' employment on children would be to conduct a study in which women are randomly assigned to various work conditions, as drug companies do with their control and experimental groups. For example, some women would be given a job and then fired from it, while others would be given a job with stability. Because, through the random assignment process, these two groups of women would be completely identical except for the types of jobs they held, we could safely say that the outcomes we find are attributable solely to the mother's job loss.

Such an experiment is unethical and unfeasible, however. Although some studies, described in Chapter 1, did randomly assign women to various conditions that encourage them to get a job, these studies did not randomly assign women to have more or less desirable *types* of jobs, or to be fired from a job, which is what we are interested in here. Therefore, in the absence of a randomized experiment, we use a variety of statistical techniques to address the issues of selection and reverse causality. We perform different analyses to reflect the variety of ways in which one could conceptualize maternal work patterns. In addition, in each set of analyses, we examine multiple facets of maternal employment.

As discussed above, maternal work can influence children's behavior in myriad ways. Our analyses adjust for these possibilities by "controlling," or holding constant with statistical techniques, only those factors that are not themselves likely to be influenced by maternal employment, specifically, child age, sex, and race, mother's age and education, home literacy environment, family structure, and father involvement in child rearing. Analyses such as these ask, "Among a group of children with the same sex, age, race, family structure, mother's education, etc., how do those whose mothers work long hours (for example), compare with those whose mothers do not?"

In our primary models reported in Chapter 3, we exclude factors that *result* from maternal job holding, since these may capture a portion of the mother's work involvement effect. However, we also estimated a set of expanded model specifications (shown in Tables A.1–A.3 in Appendix A), which use an extensive set of additional controls, not available in most other studies, to accommodate the influence of an array of other factors, including income levels and its sources, material hardship measures, child care use, residential location changes (voluntary and involuntary), neighborhood quality (neighborhood disadvantage and high crime area based on mother's reports), parental stress, social support, parenting style, and a host of mental and physical health–related characteristics of the mother.

By examining changes in the estimated impacts of mothers' work patterns as each of these sets of variables is added to the basic regression model, we gain insight into the potential linking mechanisms between mothers' work experiences and child well-being, as well as minimize the threat of selection bias. The results show that, although many of these other factors independently influence child development outcomes, the estimated impacts of mothers' employment patterns were similar in the standard and expanded models. This suggests only a minor role for potential selection bias.

Therefore, we do not present the results of these expanded analyses and instead focus on the analyses that control only for those basic characteristics of sex, age, race, family structure, and father involvement in child rearing, and mother's age and education, and home literacy environment. We next explain in more detail the statistical approaches we used.[12]

Ordinary Least Squares Models

First, we examine the basic pattern of relationships between maternal work conditions and child behavior. We use an ordinary least squares (OLS) model, which does not address the issues of selection or reverse causality noted above. Although these analyses may suffer from those problems, we include them to provide a baseline estimate of the influence of maternal employment on children. The model for our OLS analyses is shown in Equation (B.2) in Appendix B. In these models, we simply ask the following: Do behavior problems differ between children whose mothers have different work experiences? For example, how do the behavior problems of a child whose mother experiences job instability differ from those of a mother with job stability? For policymakers, an analysis such as this is useful in understanding whether some children are at risk due to their mothers' employment experiences.

Child Fixed-Effects Models

For our main analyses, we use a more rigorous approach called *child fixed effects* models (as shown in Equations [B.3]–[B.5] in Appendix B). As discussed above, when relating maternal employment to child well-being, researchers worry about the numerous ways in which mothers who work in certain types of jobs differ from those working in other jobs. Mothers experiencing job instability may have other problems, such as greater chaos in the lives, less social support, or fewer skills that result in their unstable job experiences. Such factors are likely not only associated with maternal work, but also with child behavior.

One way to address this issue is to avoid comparing mothers with different work experiences, but instead examine whether changes over time in a given mother's work experiences are linked to changes over the same period of time in her child's behavior. Such analyses compare children to themselves over time, rather than to other children with different experiences and backgrounds. Specifically we ask: How does child behavior change when a mother moves from working regular hours at one point to working unpredictable hours in the next? For policymakers, analyses such as these can pinpoint whether changes in women's employment (such as that stemming from a policy change) may lead to concurrent changes in children's behavior.

The advantage of child fixed-effects analyses is that they control for all characteristics of children, their mothers, and their families that do not change over time (and thus the term "fixed effects"), including things that researchers typically cannot measure well. This reduces, although it does not eliminate, the possibility of biased estimates; there likely still exist unmeasured factors that do change with time. For example, maternal job changes may be associated with other stressful life events. That is, there might be changes within the family (or for the child) over time that coincide with differences in maternal employment and that also affect the child's outcomes. If this is the case, then our estimate of the effect of maternal employment on children would still be somewhat biased. The fact that the standard and expanded models—which control for measured changes in mother's health and other family conditions—yielded very similar estimated impacts of changes in mother's work patterns lessen concerns that our central findings are driven by omitted variable bias.

Long-Difference Models

Other analyses use what we call long-difference models. These models allow us to examine the longer-run impacts of maternal employment patterns on child development, and to investigate whether these effects compound over time. By comparing the results of the child fixed-effects and the long-difference models, we can examine whether the influence of maternal work on child behavior represents a short-term adjustment, or whether employment effects have longer-term consequences for child well-being.

In the long-difference models, we look at the entire five waves of WES data. We count the total number of times during these five waves that a mother experienced long work hours, job instability, or unpredictable work hours, and then ask whether the total number of periods a child's mother experienced a given job condition (for example, long hours) predicts changes during that same five years in children's behavior. This allows us to examine the cumulative effect of mothers' work on children's behavior, rather than simply the effect occurring in one period, as in the child fixed-effects model. This type of model also addresses the concern about reverse causality, noted above, in that children's behavior in the first period is controlled; if such behavior had an influence on mothers' employment experiences, our long-difference model can adjust for that. The long-difference models we estimate are discussed in more detail in Appendix B. Such analyses address the following question: Does the total number of times a mother experienced a given employment condition, such as job instability, influence her children's behavior over the same period? Such analyses allow policymakers to detect whether any effects of women's employment on their children accumulate, allowing one to identify children who may be at particular risk. We expect school-related academic progress indicators such as grade repetition and placement in special education to be more sensitive to persistent exposure to working conditions over several years as opposed to exposures that occur in a single period.

Finally, we also use our longer-run models to predict child behavioral outcomes and academic progress indicators at the end of the study using the low-, medium-, and high-profile maternal work patterns experienced over the 1997–2003 period (as defined above), after controlling for the initial child outcome measure at wave 1, child age, gender, race, maternal age and education, home literacy, family structure, and living arrangements.

In Chapter 3 we present results of these analyses examining how maternal employment characteristics influence children's well-being.

Notes

1. There is some noncomparability in the characterization of involuntary job loss (i.e., being fired/laid off) because of changes in the wording of these questions across waves, so we emphasize the involuntary job loss effects in the longer-run models as opposed to the short-run models that use between-wave changes that could instead reflect changes in the wording of the survey question.
2. Our primary regression results were not sensitive to whether job changes driven by maternal concerns for child well-being were categorized as voluntary job mobility, job stability, or job instability.
3. All wages are in 1999 dollars using the CPI-U.
4. It is possible that mothers do not remember and do not accurately report their job experiences. Validation studies of survey responses to labor market information collected in this way has shown annual earnings levels and annual changes in earnings are fairly reliably reported (Bound et al. 1994). Reliability has also been shown to be fairly high in panel reports of changes in work hours, while shorter and more distant unemployment spells are more likely to be underreported. While there is possible bias in retrospective event-history reports of employment status, the direction of any resultant bias is unclear.
5. Home literacy is likely associated with skills that mothers bring to the workplace and is related to dimensions that may affect child development, so it is included as part of the education controls.
6. Because employment status changes can lead to changes in living arrangements (e.g., "doubling-up" to share expenses) and home literacy environment, we also estimated a subset of models in which the controls for living arrangements and home literacy environment are measured in the year preceding the employment pattern. We did this to ensure the estimated effects of living arrangements and home literacy are not instead capturing part of the employment pattern effects. The results were nearly identical to those reported in our main models, which supports our exogeneity assumption of family structure, living arrangements, and home literacy environment.
7. A standard deviation increase in the average *growth* rate of behavior problems is equivalent to roughly 0.20 of a standard deviation increase in the average *level* of behavior problem indices we measure. The estimated average levels and year-to-year changes in these behavioral outcomes (net of measurement error and transitory fluctuations) are based on results from unconditional hierarchical random effects models (shown in Appendix Table A4) and are also used to assess effect sizes of the maternal employment estimates in the multivariate regressions to follow.
8. Recall that in February of 1997, when the study sample was collected, all of the women were receiving welfare. That 23 percent had already left welfare within about six months shows the rapid declines in welfare receipt and rapid increases in employment rates that were characteristic of that economic period.
9. The primary reasons reported for job separations between waves 2 and 3 were 21.3 percent fired/laid off; 21.3 percent job-related quit (includes dissatisfaction with

current job, such as inadequate pay, poor working conditions, suboptimal hours, poor job match); 10.3 percent child care concern; 9.4 percent health problem; 7.6 percent transportation problem; 2.7 percent family problem/pressure; 27.4 percent other.

10. The questions used to identify women's mental health disorders came from the Composite International Diagnostic Interview developed by Kessler et al. (1994) and identifies women who met the diagnostic screening criteria for these disorders over the previous 12-month period.
11. However, as noted in Chapter 1, some researchers have shown that mothers tend to preserve much of their time with children when they leave welfare for work (Chase-Lansdale et al. 2003).
12. In all regression models, standard errors are clustered at the child level to account for the fact that each child is observed multiple times in our data.

3
The Effect of Low-Income Mothers' Employment on Children

Before presenting the results of our analysis, we first examine the simple two-way relationships between maternal employment patterns and the child behavior outcomes in which we are interested. Table 3.1 presents simple descriptive statistics for each of our child behavioral outcomes (in standard deviation units) broken down by the intensity of mother's work per week (full time vs. part time), regularity of work schedule, and type of job transition pattern experienced over the past one to two years (job stability, instability, mobility). Similarly, Table 3.2 presents the average longer-run child outcomes at the end of the survey by the mother's work experience profile over the entire study, defined along the dimensions of job quality, employment stability, and regularity of work hours (low profile, medium profile, high profile).

Children whose mothers worked full time experienced more externalizing behavior problems and were more likely to be disruptive in school relative to children whose mothers worked part time. Relative to children whose mothers worked a predictable set of hours or whose jobs were stable, those whose mothers either had fluctuating hours or experienced job instability had significantly more behavior problems overall, greater externalizing and internalizing problems, and were more likely to have school absenteeism problems. Over the longer run (Table 3.2), children whose mothers experienced the low-profile work trajectory over the period had behavior problems at the end of the survey that were roughly two-thirds of a standard deviation higher than the levels of behavior problems observed among children whose mothers experienced the high-profile work trajectory. Furthermore, 35 percent of children whose mothers experienced the low-profile work trajectory had repeated a grade by the end of the study, compared with 19 and 26 percent among children whose mothers experienced the high- and medium-profile work trajectories, respectively.

Table 3.1 Children's Outcomes Classified by Mothers' Recent Employment Histories, WES 1997–2003

	Mother's employment patterns$_{(t-1,t)}$							
Child outcome	No work	Part-time job	Full-time job	Fluctuating work hours	Regular work hours	Job stability	Job instability	Job mobility
BPI—total score (in STD units)	0.13	−0.03	−0.01	0.20**	−0.09	−0.24***	0.19	−0.15
BPI—externalizing (in STD units)	0.08	−0.09*	0.03	0.13**	−0.06	−0.23***	0.16	−0.06
BPI—internalizing (in STD units)	0.18	−0.07	−0.01	0.10**	−0.08	−0.17***	0.33	−0.05
Disruptive in school	0.28	0.33*	0.37	0.34	0.36	0.36***	0.41	0.36
School absenteeism problem	0.22	0.19	0.19	0.22**	0.19	0.15***	0.24	0.16

NOTE: The sample consists of all WES target children, where information was collected during 5 waves of interviews with mothers between 1997 and 2004. The behavioral problem indices are expressed in standard deviation units as deviations from their respective means. *indicates difference in mean of child outcome between part-time and full-time work is significant at the 10 percent level; **indicates difference in mean of child outcome between regular and fluctuating hours is significant at the 10 percent level; ***indicates difference in mean of child outcome between job stability and job instability is significant at the 10 percent level.

Table 3.2 Longer-Run Child Outcomes at End of Study Classified by Mothers' Work Experience Profiles, 1997–2003

	All child outcomes measured at wave 5						
	BPI (in STD units)	Externalizing (in STD units)	Internalizing (in STD units)	Disruptive in school (proportion)	School absenteeism (proportion)	Ever repeated grade (proportion)	Placed in special education (proportion)
Low profile (25%)	0.37*	0.34*	0.36*	0.46	0.26*	0.35*	0.20
Medium profile (50%)	−0.05	−0.03	0.00	0.41	0.24	0.26	0.20
High profile (25%)	−0.29	−0.28	−0.34	0.42	0.15	0.19	0.19

NOTE: *indicates difference in mean of child outcome between low profile and high profile is significant at the 5 percent level. *Low profile* is defined as not employed in "good" job by wave 5 and had experienced chronic job instability and/or fluctuating work hours for the vast majority of study period (i.e., either had been fired/laid off two or more times, had experienced four or more voluntary job-to-nonemployment transitions, and/or had two or more years of fluctuating work hours over the seven-year study period). *Medium profile* is defined as not employed in "good" job by wave 5, some job instability or fluctuating work hours, but not persistently so to be categorized as low profile, and improvement in work trajectory not great enough to be categorized as high profile. *High profile* is defined as employed in "good" job by wave 5 and had experienced employment stability and regular work hours for the vast majority of study period (i.e., had not been fired/laid off, had experienced three or fewer voluntary job-to-nonemployment transitions, and one or fewer periods of fluctuating work hours over the seven-year study period). The behavioral problem indices are expressed in standard deviation units as deviations from their respective means.

Of course, mothers who have different employment patterns are different from one another in ways, beyond simply their work experiences, that may also contribute to the differences in their children's developmental outcomes. Table 3.3 highlights this point by presenting a series of family characteristics broken down by the same maternal employment patterns as presented in Table 3.1. For example, compared with mothers who experienced job stability, mothers who experienced job instability, on average, had less family income and earnings, were less educated, were more likely to receive welfare or experience food insufficiency, have been evicted at some time in the past year, and had worse health.

We would expect all these other factors to affect child well-being, independent of maternal employment. The remainder of this analysis aims to examine whether it is the maternal employment pattern itself that leads to the child's disadvantage, or these other differences in family characteristics. To put a human face to the numbers, we draw on in-depth interviews with women in the WES whom Kristin Seefeldt interviewed for a qualitative analysis of women's work experiences. Seefeldt and her colleagues spent hours in the homes of these women, talking about work, family, and life after welfare reform (Seefeldt 2008).

THE JUGGLING ACT

Olivia, a mother in her early thirties takes a call at work from her son's school: "Alex has been in a fight and is being suspended for the week. Please come and pick him up right away." Olivia glances up at the big board. Forty calls are on hold waiting for help. She takes off her headset and goes in search of her supervisor.

"Can't anybody else go and pick him up?" her boss asks impatiently. He himself has no children. "Well, I'm his mother," Olivia says, "and they called me to go and pick him up. I can come back and finish out my shift, you know. I've seen other people do it on numerous occasions, and I've been here five years."

Her supervisor, unfortunately, does not see it that way. He demands that she call someone else to pick him up. What he didn't understand,

Olivia tells the interviewer in Seefeldt's study, is that "when the school calls and says 'pick him up,' that means come and get your child. They don't want to hear, okay, you're at work and you can't go and get him. They know I'm at work because they called me at work!"

It took Olivia an hour to find someone to pick him up. After calling her mother and her brother to no avail, she found one of her friends who could go to the school. "You know," she told Seefeldt, "it's not like I live in a different city and I would have had to drive 30, 40 minutes. We're talking 5, 10 minutes and then dropping him off somewhere."

These are the balls that single mothers with children must juggle when they go to work. The phone calls from school that a child is in trouble are not infrequent for many of the women in the WES sample, nor are instances of frustration and worry among mothers because their children are acting out or, in some cases, withdrawing into themselves.

Like Olivia's son, a sizable share of children, as noted in the prior chapter, were disruptive in school or were frequently absent, placed in special education, or held back to repeat a grade. In addition to school issues, children were more likely than national averages to act out, fight, or destroy things (although they did not differ from national averages on measures of being depressed or withdrawn).

The strains of the working poor, living paycheck to paycheck, being worried about paying the heating bill or filling the car's gas tank, can tax anyone. Add to this the weight of raising children as a single parent—especially when children display difficult behavior—tempers can snap, attention can be distracted, and time can be pinched. When work hours are unpredictable and child care is inflexible or nonexistent, children can be left to their own devices or be charged with the care of their younger siblings. All of these factors can create or exacerbate children's behavior problems.

These effects are shown in our main set of results, which are presented in Tables 3.4 (OLS results), 3.5 (child fixed-effect results), and 3.6 (longer-run results). Looking across these tables, certain patterns emerge. Overall, we see that job instability and fluctuating work hours are associated with increased child behavior problems, as the story of Olivia and her children underscore.

Table 3.3 Other Characteristics of Childhood Families Classified by Mothers' Recent Employment Histories, WES 1997–2003[a]

	Mother's employment patterns$_{(t-1,t)}$							
	No work	Part-time job	Full-time job	Fluctuating work hours	Regular work hours	Job stability	Job instability	Job mobility
Used paid child care services$_{t-1,t}$ (for any child)	0.03	0.23*	0.28	0.22*	0.27	0.25	0.24	0.31
Income sources and material hardship								
Family income-to-needs ratio$_{t-1,t}$	0.84	1.05*	1.29	1.12**	1.22	1.39***	1.10	1.30
Maternal earnings$_{t-1,t}$ ($)	0.00	494*	960	676**	804	1173***	525	994
Received welfare$_{t-1,t}$	0.71	0.50*	0.28	0.42**	0.35	0.19***	0.35	0.22
Food insufficiency index$_{t-1,t}$	0.29	0.23*	0.18	0.23**	0.19	0.18***	0.21	0.18
Residential mobility/ instability variables								
Moved$_{t-1,t}$	0.38	0.41*	0.46	0.43	0.44	0.35***	0.51	0.42
Evicted$_{t-1,t}$	0.08	0.09*	0.07	0.09	0.07	0.04***	0.12	0.05
Neighborhood disadvantage (crime)$_{W1}$	0.55	0.48*	0.54	0.55**	0.50	0.50	0.53	0.49
Parental characteristics								
Parental stress index$_t$	22.29	21.68	22.01	21.82	21.90	22.01	21.90	22.09
Stressful life events index$_{W1}$	2.09	2.16	2.25	2.37**	2.18	2.11***	2.32	2.10

Social support index$_{W1}$	4.27	4.35	4.32	4.22**	4.36	4.43***	4.28	4.39
White	0.44	0.51*	0.40	0.40**	0.46	0.47	0.43	0.45
Black	0.56	0.49*	0.60	0.60**	0.54	0.53	0.57	0.55
Maternal education								
HS dropout	0.41	0.27	0.24	0.28	0.24	0.17***	0.30	0.20
HS grad$_{t}$	0.34	0.38	0.39	0.38	0.39	0.40	0.40	0.35
Some college$_{t}$	0.25	0.36	0.37	0.34	0.37	0.43***	0.30	0.46
Home literacy environment index$_{W1}$	2.91	3.13*	3.25	3.21	3.20	3.34***	3.10	3.19
Never married mom$_{W1}$	0.58	0.58*	0.64	0.60	0.62	0.62	0.64	0.58
Father involvement index$_{W1}$	10.05	9.68	9.54	9.91**	9.49	9.87***	9.33	9.75
Harsh parenting index$_{W1}$	13.39	14.33	14.42	14.42	14.37	14.34	14.44	14.46
Mother's alcohol or drug use problem$_{W1}$	0.19	0.23	0.21	0.23	0.21	0.19***	0.24	0.21
Mother's physical health problem$_{W1}$	0.37	0.17	0.16	0.20**	0.15	0.13***	0.19	0.15
Mother's probable diagnosis major depression$_{W1}$	0.30	0.22	0.21	0.24**	0.21	0.17***	0.24	0.22

NOTE: *Indicates difference in mean between part-time and full-time work is significant at the 10% level; **indicates difference in mean between regular and fluctuating hours is significant at the 10% level; ***indicates difference in mean between job stability and job instability is significant at the 10% level.[a] The sample consists of all WES target children, where information was collected during five waves of interviews with mothers between 1997 and 2004.

Table 3.4 The Effects of Maternal Employment Patterns on Child Well-Being: All Behavior Problems, WES 1997–2003

	Dependent variables—child outcomes$_t$				
	OLS			Probit models (marginal effects)	
	Behavior problem index$_t$	Externalizing scale$_t$	Internalizing scale$_t$	Prob(disruptive in school)$_t$	Prob(school absenteeism)$_t$
Maternal employment-related variables	(1)	(2)	(3)	(4)	(5)
Years of work experience$_t$	−0.09**	−0.02**	−0.02*	0.00	0.00
(ref cat: Job Stability)	(0.04)	(0.01)	(0.01)	(0.00)	(0.00)
Cumulative years of job instability$_{W0,t}$	0.55***	0.13**	0.20***	0.04***	0.04***
	(0.16)	(0.05)	(0.06)	(0.01)	(0.01)
Cumulative years of voluntary job mobility$_{W0,t}$	0.06	−0.01	0.01	0.00	−0.04
	(0.23)	(0.07)	(0.09)	(0.02)	(0.02)
Cumulative years of full-time work$_{W0,t}$	0.11	0.01	0.03	0.01	0.00
	(0.13)	(0.04)	(0.05)	(0.01)	(0.01)
Cumulative years of fluctuating work hours$_{W0,t}$	0.30*	0.09*	0.06	−0.01	0.02*
	(0.18)	(0.06)	(0.07)	(0.02)	(0.01)
Child-year observations	1,572	2,256	2,249	2,115	1,068
Number of children	520	575	575	564	456

NOTE: ***p<0.01, **p<0.05, *p<0.10. All models include controls for child age, gender, race, maternal age, maternal education, home literacy environment scale, family structure, and father involvement in child rearing. These effects are suppressed in the table to conserve space. In these analyses, the coefficient on "years of work experience" represents mothers working and experiencing job stability, relative to those who did not work. The coefficients on cumulative years of job instability and voluntary job mobility are in reference to job stability. So, for example, the coefficient on "cumulative years of job instability" indicates the change in children's behavior associated with an additional year of work experience in an unstable job relative to that work experience in a stable job. To understand the influence on children of the movement from nonwork to a year of work experience in an unstable job, one would sum the coefficients on "years of work experience" and "cumulative years of job instability." Because nearly all mothers worked at some point over the past year, the work versus nonworking comparison is less useful than is characterizing the nature and pattern of employment, and identifying differential effects in the type of maternal work involvement on child well-being. Robust standard errors in parentheses (clustered on child).

Table 3.5 The Effects of Changes in Maternal Employment Patterns on Changes in Child Well-Being: WES 1997–2003

	First-difference models: dependent variables—Δ child outcomes$_{t-1,t}$				
Maternal employment-related variables	Δ Behavior problem index$_{t-1,t}$ (1)	Δ Externalizing scale$_{t-1,t}$ (2)	Δ Internalizing scale$_{t-1,t}$ (3)	Δ Prob (disruptive in school)$_{t-1,t}$ (4)	Δ Prob(school absenteeism)$_{t-1,t}$ (5)
Worked$_{t-1,t}$	−0.43*	−0.22**	−0.12	−0.01	−0.08
(ref cat: Job Stability)	(0.29)	(0.09)	(0.10)	(0.04)	(0.06)
Worked$_{t-1,t}$*job instability$_{t-1,t}$	0.50*	0.13*	0.23***	0.00	0.03
	(0.27)	(0.07)	(0.09)	(0.03)	(0.04)
Worked$_{t-1,t}$*voluntary job mobility$_{t-1,t}$	0.45*	0.03	0.13	0.05	0.00
	(0.27)	(0.09)	(0.10)	(0.04)	(0.04)
Δ Full-time work hours$_{t-1,t}$	−0.02	0.12*	0.00	0.02	0.03
	(0.22)	(0.07)	(0.08)	(0.03)	(0.04)
Δ Fluctuating work hours$_{t-1,t}$	0.45*	0.11*	0.16**	−0.03	0.03
	(0.23)	(0.07)	(0.08)	(0.03)	(0.05)
Child-year observations	1,047	1,666	1,656	1,478	744
Number of children	457	524	523	497	408

NOTE: ***p<0.01, **p<0.05, *p<0.10. In these analyses, the coefficient on "worked" represents mothers working and experiencing job stability between waves, relative to those who did not work. As with the OLS models, the coefficients on job instability are in reference to those who worked and had job stability. So, for example, the coefficient on "worked*job instability" indicates the change in children's behavior associated with movement from a stable job to an unstable job between waves. To understand the influence on children of the movement from nonwork to an unstable job, one would sum the coefficients on "worked" and "worked*job instability." Because nearly all mothers worked at some point over the past year, the work versus nonworking comparison is less useful than is characterizing the nature and pattern of employment, and identifying differential effects in the type of maternal work involvement on child well-being. All models include controls for changes in child age, maternal education, home literacy environment scale, family structure, father involvement in child rearing, and number of months between waves. These effects are suppressed in the table to conserve space. Robust standard errors in parentheses (clustered on child).

Table 3.6 The Longer-Run Impacts of Maternal Employment Patterns on Child Well-Being: WES 1997–2003

	Dependent variables—Δ child outcomes$_{W1,W5}$						
Maternal employment-related variables	Behavior problem index$_{W5}$ (1)	Externalizing scale$_{W5}$ (2)	Internalizing scale$_{W5}$ (3)	Prob (disruptive in school)$_{W5}$ (4)	Prob(school absenteeism)$_{W5}$ (5)	Prob(ever repeated a grade)$_{W3-W5}$ (6)	Prob(ever placed in special ed.)$_{W3-W5}$ (7)
Δ No. of months worked$_{W1,W5}$	0.02	0.01	0.01	0.00	0.00	0.00	0.00
	(0.03)	(0.04)	(0.03)	(0.00)	(0.00)	(0.00)	(0.00)
Δ No. of involuntary job-to-nonemployment transitions$_{W1,W5}$	0.80**	0.89*	1.13***	0.10**	0.01	0.01	0.02
	(0.40)	(0.54)	(0.38)	(0.05)	(0.03)	(0.03)	(0.02)
Δ No. of voluntary job-to-nonemployment transitions$_{W1,W5}$	0.36*	0.45*	0.32*	0.04*	0.02	0.03**	0.01
	(0.20)	(0.26)	(0.19)	(0.02)	(0.01)	(0.01)	(0.01)
Δ No. of voluntary job-to-job transitions$_{W1,W5}$	−0.01	−0.06	0.18	−0.04	−0.01	−0.02	−0.02
	(0.27)	(0.36)	(0.26)	(0.03)	(0.02)	(0.02)	(0.02)
Δ Full-time work hours$_{W1,W5}$	1.10**	1.00*	0.73*	0.04	0.03	0.06*	0.06*
	(0.43)	(0.57)	(0.40)	(0.05)	(0.03)	(0.04)	(0.03)
Δ Full-time work hours$_{W1,W5}$ *reading/writing/computer use	−0.91	−0.49	−0.06	−0.07	−0.10**	−0.05	−0.03
	(0.67)	(0.90)	(0.64)	(0.08)	(0.05)	(0.05)	(0.04)

Δ No. of yrs spent working fluctuating hours$_{W1,W5}$	0.58** (0.28)	0.62* (0.37)	0.62** (0.27)	−0.01 (0.03)	0.06*** (0.02)	0.04* (0.02)	0.03* (0.02)
Two-year average transition probability (conditional on not occurring in prior periods)	—	—	—	—	—	0.1254	0.1381
No. of children	280	278	278	298	360	332	338

NOTE: ***p<0.01, **p<0.05, *p<0.10. All models include controls for wave 1 of child outcome, as well as for gender, child age, and changes in maternal education, home literacy environment scale, family structure, father involvement in child rearing, and whether worked between waves. These effects are suppressed in the table to conserve space. Models in columns (6) and (7) are conditional on the child previously not held back a grade or placed in special education, respectively, prior to the final two survey waves. Standard errors in parentheses.

UNPREDICTABLE WORK SCHEDULES ASSOCIATED WITH BEHAVIOR PROBLEMS

Even after five years on the job with steady advancement, Olivia still never knows what her weekly work schedule will be. She started at the bank as a call operator routing incoming calls, making $8.00 an hour. Driven to do better, she signed up for all the training she could manage and steadily advanced to her position as a commercial services customer representative at $11.00, or approximately $23,000 for a full-time position. A 3 percent raise came with the latest training in technical support, and she now occasionally fields calls from customers who are having trouble with the financial services software the bank sells.

It's a stressful job, she says, because "you are trying to please other people. You're trying to meet the bank's need, which is making money, and you're also trying to satisfy your client." She fields approximately 200 calls a day from people with problems or complaints—needless to say, not always a happy bunch. Yet she is not unhappy with her work. She likes her colleagues and appreciates the opportunities for advancement. However, the hours, she says, are brutal. She works typically 50 hours per week, and each week the hours change.

"It's always full-time hours," she says "but you don't get to choose your schedule. Some weeks it's 8:00 a.m. to 5:00 p.m., or I could work a schedule where I'm working 10:30 a.m. to 7:00 p.m., or I would work 12:00 p.m. to 9:00 p.m. Everything is different every week, so you never really know what you're working until you get your schedule, and they usually give us two weeks' notice."

This fluctuating schedule makes it nearly impossible to attend her children's school events, or even get them dinner in the evenings. "It's hard for me to adjust to that concept, every day not knowing when you're going to work," she says. "It makes it hard, and that creates a problem because you need to be there.

"Not having enough time to spend with them, that's the most difficult," she says of her children. "They try to be understanding about things like school and things of that nature, but I just think it's real difficult for them to understand every time I can't make it, or, 'No you can't go because no one's there to drive you or pick you up.' Things like that."

Like many working mothers, Olivia sometimes feels like an island. "I feel like a person who doesn't have kids can't understand if you need to call in with a sick kid. I always tell my supervisor, 'You're 25, you do not have kids.' If you have children, when they're sick, you don't always want to put them off on a family member. You want to be there for your child no matter if they're 10 or 12, you know? I think it's hard for a person who doesn't have children to understand the responsibilities of a person with children."

In some cases, the toll on children who lack supervision can be serious, particularly if they are growing up in rough neighborhoods or in already precarious circumstances. The early, negative results of welfare reform on teens noted in Chapter 1, for example, point to the lack of supervision by working mothers as one potential reason for the more frequent school and behavior problems among them.

Our own findings suggest that although working, as opposed to not working at all, is associated with fewer behavior problems among children, the type of work matters. We find that how mothers' work experiences influence child behavior outcomes depends on the stability of that work in terms of both hours and job transitions. We find that children whose mothers experienced greater job instability, or who, like Olivia, spent more time working in jobs with fluctuating hours, have consistently worse behavior problems on average at the end of the period (relative to children whose mothers experienced stable work patterns).

The negative impact on children of fluctuating work hours is shown in our OLS (Table 3.4), child fixed-effect (Table 3.5), and longer-run regression models (Table 3.6). In our fixed-effects regression models, we find that when a mother moves from having stable, predictable hours to fluctuating hours, her children's behavior problems increase. (We also find that behavior problems improve when a mother moves from not working to working in a stable job.) Olivia's case points to the possible reasons for these negative consequences.

In Figures 3.1–3.3, we take the results of the child fixed-effect analyses and show the effect on children's behavior of changes in mothers' work experiences. Because we are using several different measures of children's behavioral adjustment, each with a different range of values, in these figures we use a standardized way of measuring the average dif-

Figure 3.1 Effects of Mothers' Fluctuating Work Hours on Child Behavior Outcomes, Child Fixed-Effects Results

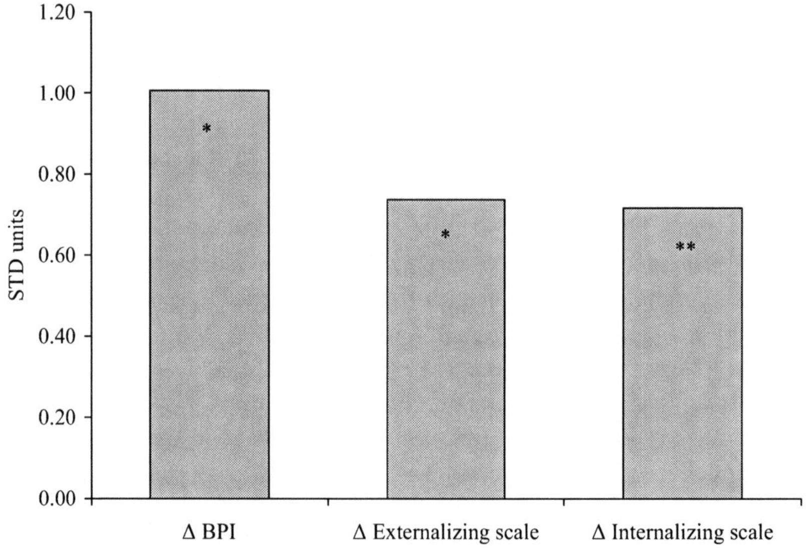

NOTE: **$p<0.05$; *$p<0.10$. These results are the estimated effects of a work status change to fluctuating work hours on the change in child behavioral outcomes from one year to the next.

ference in child outcomes between mothers who experienced a different type of work condition, which allows us to compare the magnitudes of effects across different behavioral outcome measures. Specifically, the increase in behavior problems due to mothers' work is represented as a fraction of the standard deviation, or variation, in the average year-to-year change in behavior problems for each measure.

As summarized in Figure 3.1, we find that the impact of fluctuating weekly work hours, as Olivia experienced, represents approximately one full standard deviation increase in the average growth rate of behavior problems. The combination of maternal job instability and fluctuating work hours together have estimated effects on child well-being that are equivalent to a 47 percent standard deviation increase in the level of internalizing behavior problems. While a single year-to-year change in the growth rate of behavior problems, on average, represents a relatively small impact on the overall level of problem behaviors, such changes

Figure 3.2 Longer-Run Impacts of Mothers' Fluctuating Work Hours on Child Behavior Outcomes at End of Survey, Longer-Run Model Results

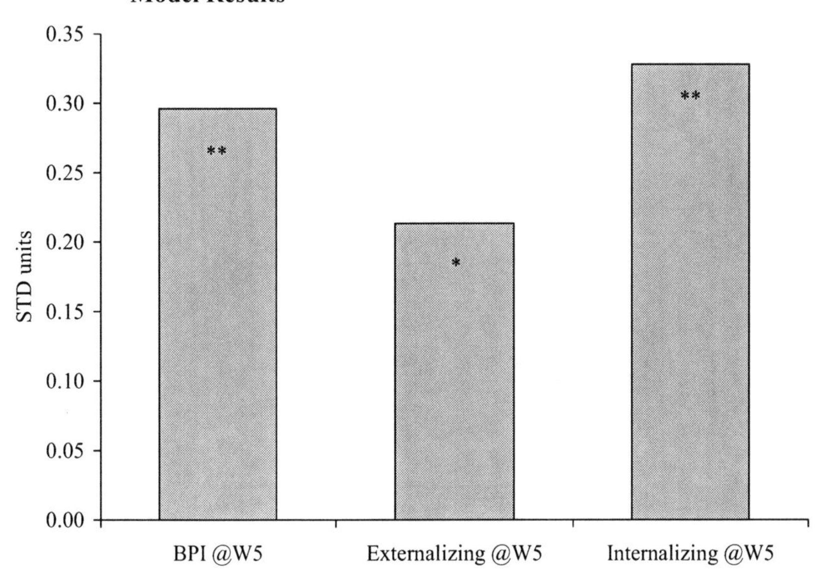

NOTE: **p<0.05; *p<0.10 (for both figures). These results are the average estimated effects on child behavioral outcomes at the end of the survey that result from a mother spending two additional years in a job with fluctuating work hours.

in the growth rate of problem behaviors could accumulate over several years to yield significant impacts on the level of problem behaviors.

To interpret the increases in child behavior problems represented by these effects, it is useful to consider a child who, if her mother experienced stable work patterns, would achieve about the average behavior score of all children in the sample. What would be the result, then, of an increase of one-fifth of a standard deviation in the level of internalizing problem behaviors because of the mother's movement to fluctuating work hours in the subsequent period (i.e., the average increase in the level of internalizing behavior problems among children when mothers experienced fluctuating work hours)? That child would move from the 50th percentile of all children up to the 58th percentile in exhibiting problem behaviors, thus surpassing an additional 8 percent of children in problematic behavior (after a single period of exposure). Clearly, a

Figure 3.3 Effects of Mothers' Job Instability (relative to job stability) on Child Behavior Outcomes, Child Fixed-Effects Results

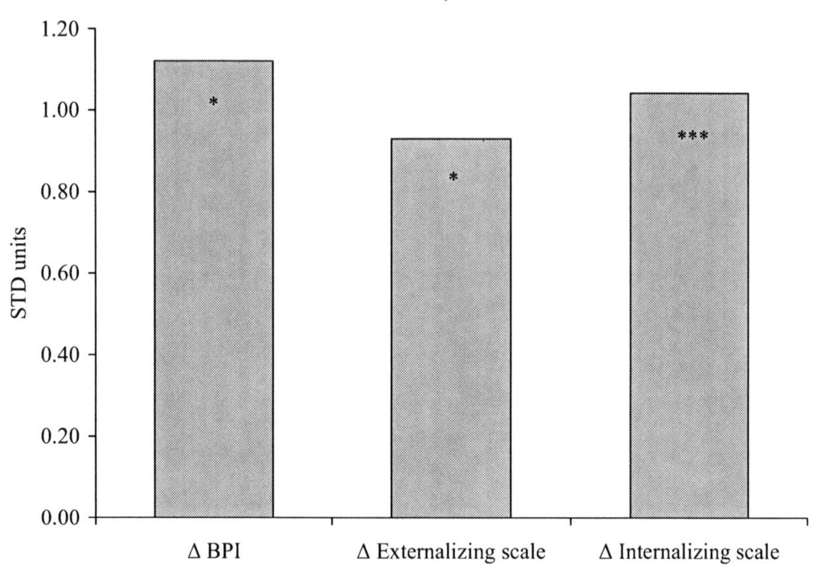

NOTE: ***p<0.01; *p<0.10. These results are the estimate effects of maternal job instability (relative to job stability) experienced over the past year on the change in child behavior outcomes from year to year.

one-fifth of one standard deviation increase can accumulate and lead to a considerable increase in behavior problems over time.

Because behavior problems are likely to develop over time, in our longer-run models we also examined the compounding effects of a mother's work on children's behavior at home and in school between wave 1 in 1997 and wave 5 in 2003 (Table 3.6).[1] In that analysis, we find that the number of years spent working in jobs with fluctuating schedules has significant impacts on child internalizing and externalizing behavioral issues over time (controlling for the child's relevant initial assessment of each outcome at wave 1). In particular, as shown in Figure 3.2, a child's additional two years of exposure to mother's fluctuating work hours leads to about 0.30 of a standard deviation increase in the level of behavior problems by the end of the survey. For the average child, this effect size would move the child from the 50th percentile of all children up to the 62nd percentile in exhibiting problem behaviors, thus surpassing an additional 12 percent of children in problematic behavior. Furthermore, an additional year spent working fluctuating hours is associated with a six-percentage-point increase in the likelihood of school absenteeism problems at the end of the study, as well as about a four-percentage-point increase in the probability of repeating a grade or being placed in special education. Thus, the longer-run impacts of mothers' fluctuating work hours are associated with a 20 percent increase in the likelihood of a child repeating a grade and a 24 percent increase in the likelihood of a child being placed in special education over the final two waves of the study.

JOB CHURN AND ASSOCIATED RISKS FOR CHILDREN

What Olivia has going for her is a fairly long tenure at the same job. Her employer is realizing her commitment and, as an employee, Olivia is becoming more reliable and steady, which earns her incremental, albeit rather small, raises. In contrast, women who frequently experience job instability and who consequently bounce from job to job, and those who lose jobs due to being laid off or fired, are more likely to add children's behavioral issues to their list of stresses. In the WES sample, about 35 percent of mothers lost a job due to being fired or laid off at least once over the seven years of the study, and 10 percent lost two more jobs for such involuntary reasons. Whether for voluntary or involuntary reasons (i.e., whether women initiated the job separation due to dissatisfaction with working conditions or the job separation occurred due to being fired or laid off), 82 percent of mothers who worked at some point over the study experienced at least one job-to-nonemployment transition with an intervening spell of nonemployment lasting a month or more for reasons that were not driven primarily by maternal concerns for child care over the seven years of the study. Twenty-five percent of mothers who worked at some point over the study experienced one job-to-nonemployment transition, 17 percent experienced two such transitions, 15 percent experienced three, and 25 percent experienced four or more episodes of job instability.

The median job duration for women in the WES was seven months, and only about a third of jobs lasted a year or more. Job transitions observed in the sample are disproportionately comprised of job-to-nonemployment transitions, as opposed to voluntary job-to-job transitions, which are associated with wage gains. Even in the economic boom of the late 1990s, the job turnover rates among jobs held by the WES sample of respondents were substantially higher than that observed for less-skilled workers more generally in national samples.[2] Thus, the incidence of job instability witnessed among our sample of former/current welfare recipients represent significantly higher turnover rates than is observed among non-college-educated, young women who have never been welfare recipients.

The economic recession that occurred in 2001 during the midpoint of our study highlighted the sensitivity of low-income women's job transition patterns to changes in labor market demand conditions. Less-educated workers are more affected by economic downturns than are more-educated workers—they are often the last hired and first fired. When unemployment rises, less-educated workers are more likely to lose their jobs, to move into part-time work, or to leave the labor force entirely. Unemployment rates in Michigan reached a low of 3.7 percent in 2000 but then rose significantly during the economic slowdown at the turn of the century, to 7.1 percent in 2003. Prior work using these data has demonstrated that a one-percentage-point increase in the local unemployment rate increases the monthly probability of being laid off/fired by about 10 percent (Johnson 2006). Such involuntary job loss can lead to more frequent residential moves, which, as we show later, has important adverse consequences for the well-being of children in low-income families. Prior research with these data also demonstrates that job loss sharply increases the annual probability that children will move out of their neighborhoods (Allard, Johnson, and Danziger 2007).

The fixed-effect and longer-term analysis leaves little doubt that job instability contributes significantly to behavior problems in children, independent of other factors such as income, evictions, family structure, and mother's mental health. (See results in Tables 3.5 and 3.6 and Tables A.2 and A.3 in Appendix A for fixed-effects results.) The fixed-effects results are summarized in Figure 3.3. The magnitude of the effects indicates that job instability leads to a full standard deviation increase in the growth rate of behavior problems. Moreover, the effect size of job instability on the growth rate of internalizing behavior problems translates into 0.27 of a standard deviation increase in the level of internalizing behavior problems. For the average child, this means that he or she would move from the 50th percentile of all children up to the 61st percentile in exhibiting internalizing problem behaviors when a mother experiences job instability, thus surpassing an additional 11 percent of children in problematic behavior. Effect sizes on the order of 0.10, 0.20, or 0.30 may not seem to be large increases in the overall level of problem behavior for an individual child due to a single-period exposure to mothers' unstable work patterns; however, for a population of children whose mothers experience these unstable work patterns with some persistence (as noted above, a full 25 percent of our mothers experienced four or more episodes of job instability), they can be quite substantial.

While a single job loss over the period is associated with a much smaller detrimental impact on child behavior outcomes in the longer run, these negative effects intensify with multiple occurrences of instability accumulated over time. Results from these longer-run analyses are summarized in Figure 3.4, and shown in Tables 3.4 and A.3. Because all transitions can be difficult for children, we compare the effect of involuntary job separations due to being fired or laid off to that of voluntary job-to-nonemployment transitions typically initiated by women due to dissatisfaction with working conditions. Being laid off or fired leads to significantly greater (roughly 2–4 times greater) child behavior problems, particularly internalizing behavior problems, and a greater likelihood the child is disruptive in school than when mothers' jobs change by choice.[3] For example, although an additional voluntary shift from working to not working is associated with a four-percentage-point increase in the likelihood of the child being disruptive in school at wave 5, being laid off or fired is associated with a 10-percentage-point increase in the probability of being disruptive in school at that time.

Additionally, the results indicate that the significant difference in child behavior problems between those whose mothers experienced two involuntary job separations compared with children whose mothers had never been fired or laid off over the study period amounts to roughly one-half of one standard deviation disparity in behavior prob-

Figure 3.4 Longer-Run Impacts of Maternal Employment on Child Behavior Outcomes at End of Survey, Longer-Run Model Results

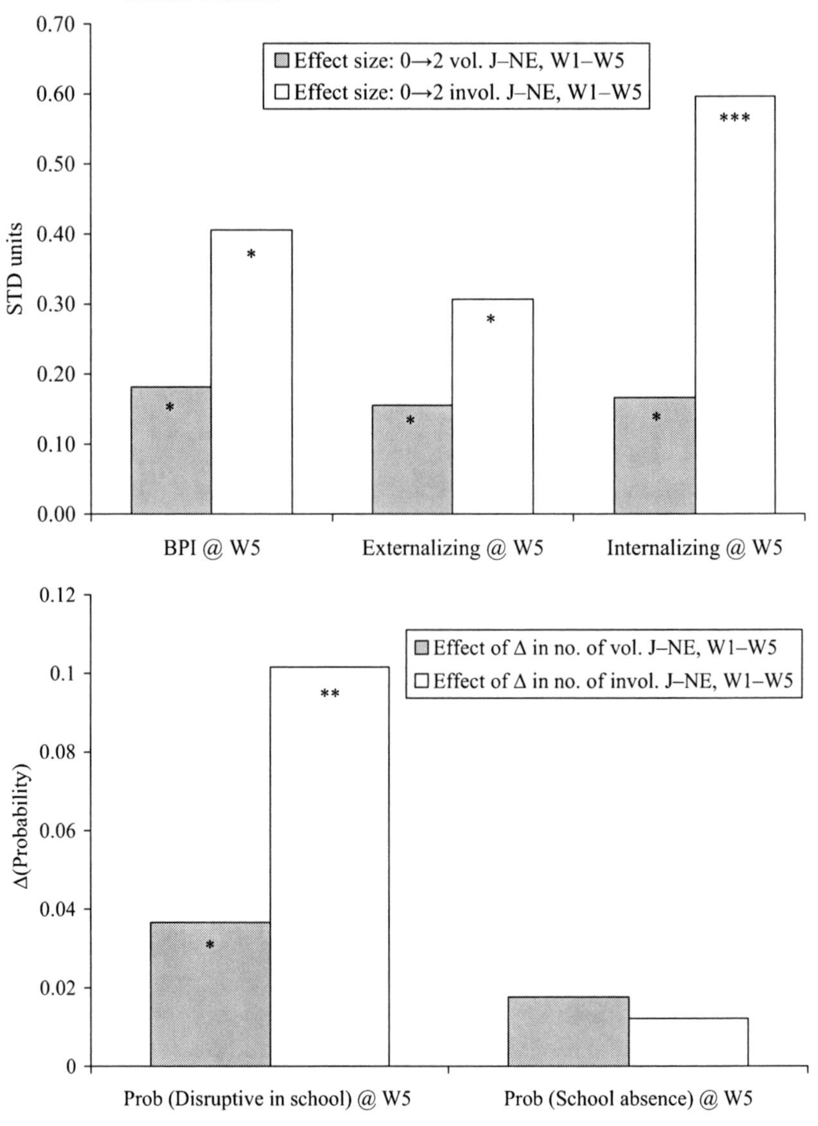

NOTE: ***p<0.01; **p<0.05; *p<0.10. The top figure shows the estimated effects of an additional two voluntary vs. involuntary job-to-nonemployment transitions (W1–W5) on child behavior outcomes at the wave 5 survey. The bottom figure shows the estimated effects of each additional voluntary vs. involuntary job-to-nonemployment transition on the likelihood the child exhibits disruptive behavior problems in school and school absenteeism problems, respectively, at the wave 5 survey.

lems by the end of the survey (more specifically, these effect sizes are 0.41, 0.31, and 0.60 of a standard deviation in the total behavior problem index, externalizing scale, and internalizing scale, respectively). To put the magnitude of these effects in perspective, consider that in the absence of these involuntary job losses, a reduction of half a standard deviation in the overall level of behavior problems would move children who were originally average (which is also the 50 percent point on these distributions) down to about the 31st percentile point in problem behaviors. Thus, a child whose level of behavior problems initially exceeded half this low-income population of children would now exhibit fewer behavior problems than 69 percent of the sample of children if his or her mother had never experienced being laid off or fired.

Seefeldt's interviews again bring this toll to life. Trudy is a mother with two children—a toddler and a 10-year-old. She has held 11 jobs over four years, with bouts of unemployment in between. She worked on a temp job on an assembly line before being laid off and moving to another job the temp agency found for her. When she lost that job, she filled in as a housekeeper. She then took a job as a dishwasher and cleaner in a restaurant. Her low wages forced her to look for another job, which she found as a cashier at a supermarket.

As her job instability continued over the course of the study, her oldest son Eric's behavior got progressively worse. Eric, Trudy reports, was diagnosed with attention deficit/hyperactivity disorder. She answers yes to the following list of questions: Eric does not get along with teachers and is disobedient at school; he rarely follows family rules; often cheats and lies; requires frequent disciplining; is sometimes impulsive and breaks things deliberately. Even though Trudy often is forced to take away Eric's privileges in an attempt to discipline him, she says nothing works. She says Eric rarely feels sorry for misbehaving. These outward expressions may also be hiding some internalizing troubles. Her son, Trudy tells the interviewer, also complains that no one loves him.

From the first interview to the last, Trudy's story reveals a deteriorating home situation with her son. As his behavior deteriorated, Trudy's financial situation remained highly precarious and her jobs were short and frequent. She also moved often, including a move from Michigan to Texas and back, and was living in a different apartment for each of the five interviews. The homes were often cold and chaotic. The strain eventually became such that she asked her own mother to take Eric. Eric moved in with his grandmother in 2000, three years into the study. As our analyses show, moves like these, as well as evictions and other housing instability, are highly correlated in our study with job instability.

While we cannot say that Trudy's string of unstable, low-paying jobs was the only reason for Eric's behavior problems, we can say that her job instability accounted for a substantial share of the growth of his problem behaviors (independent of the impacts of changes in living arrangements and residential moves). It is worth emphasizing that the worsening behavior depicted in stories like Eric's coincided with his mother's periods of volatile work patterns (as opposed to persistent behavior problems continuing over the study period in the absence of these work patterns). Likewise, given our results, we can say with some confidence that the other possibility is not instead the case: that Eric's behavior caused Trudy to lose her jobs. The interview notes show no indication from Trudy that her job loss was due to Eric's behavior, which seems to add support, indirectly at least, to our findings that job instability is a significant reason for behavior problems. Instead, she talked of low pay, frequent misunderstandings, conflict, and boredom that led her to quit or be fired. As our results and Seefeldt's interviews show, job loss is stressful, particularly when there are children to feed and clothe, and no spouse or partner is there to cushion the income loss.

Long Hours at Low Pay Associated with Child Behavior Problems

The analyses we just presented may mask the fact that, for some mothers, sustained employment leads to upward mobility, while for many others it represents the first in a succession of dead-end jobs. We therefore investigated whether the effect of full-time work on children differs depending on whether the job leads to greater wage growth in subsequent years.

For example, jobs requiring more cognitive skills—in particular, a daily demand for reading or writing and computer use—have significantly higher prospects for wage growth and have been shown to be primary pathways to upward mobility, independent of the characteristics of the workers who fill these jobs. Moreover, these differences in wage growth opportunities across jobs frequently determine whether a woman leaves a job (independent of worker characteristics) (Johnson 2006).

In our longer-run analyses (Table 3.6), we find that working full time in jobs that require more cognitive skills is not associated with children's behavior problems; this is likely because women in such jobs are more likely to experience wage growth and less likely to experience job instability in future periods than are women in less cognitively demanding jobs. However, working full time in jobs that do not require those cognitive skills is associated with significantly worse child behavioral outcomes by the end of the period.

Increases in earnings among the mothers in our sample over the study period were driven disproportionately by increases in the number of weeks worked per year and the number of hours worked, as opposed to increases in the wages earned per hour. Wage growth opportunities enable greater earnings over time without necessarily having to sacrifice the quantity or quality of time spent with the child, whereas increases in work hours may constrain the quality of time spent with the child. Thus, the route that provides the primary source of earnings growth may have very different ramifications for child well-being. The data bear out this reality.

As shown in Figure 3.5, we find that changes to full-time work in less cognitively demanding jobs (which offer more limited wage growth opportunities) are associated with greater externalizing and internalizing behavioral problems for children. It also has ramifications for school performance. Over time, it is associated with a six-percentage-point increase in both the probability of a child repeating a grade and the probability that a child is placed in special education between waves 3 and 5 (as shown in Figure 3.6). The average proportion of children who repeated a grade or were placed in special education over a two-year period (conditional on it not occurring in earlier periods) was roughly 10 percent for each of these longer-run academic progress indicators. When women like Olivia work longer hours (more than 35 per week) in less cognitively demanding jobs (which offer more limited wage growth opportunities), the risk for behavior problems among their children increases significantly. These worsening behavior and school problems

Figure 3.5 Differential Effects of Mothers' Increase to Full-Time Work by Wage Growth Potential on Child Behavior Outcomes at End of Survey, Longer-Run Model Results

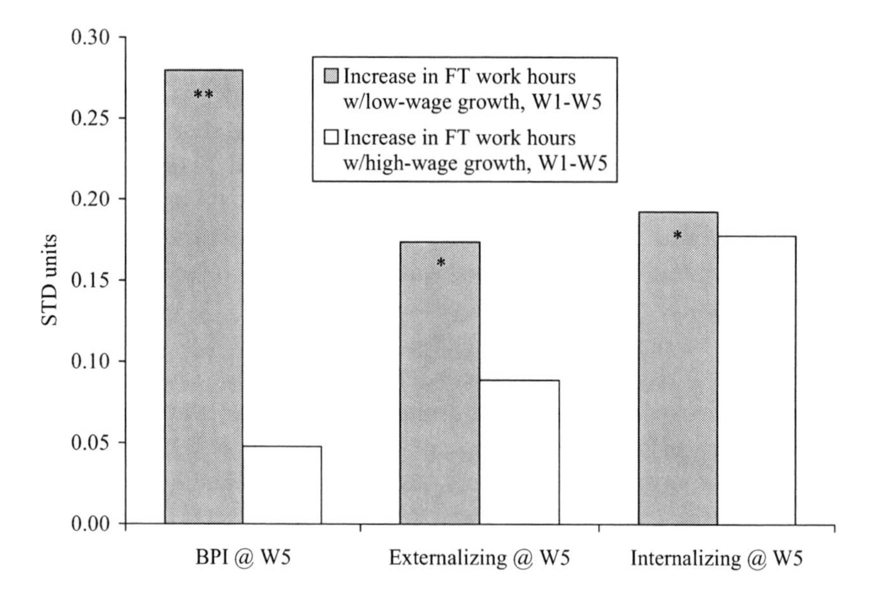

NOTE: $**p<0.05$; $*p<0.10$.

were not evident when a mother increased her work hours in more cognitively demanding jobs that offer higher wage growth prospects.

Sarah, for example, another of Seefeldt's interviewees, has two school-aged children who are seemingly doing quite well in school, even though Sarah works full time and wishes she could be there more for them. She works at the deli counter in a local grocery store chain. The union job is secure and steady, allowing her to work daily from 8:00 to 4:30, with the occasional opportunity for overtime. Her wages have grown steadily during her six years on the job. "The reason why I think my job is good," she says, "is because when I started, I got $4.25 an hour, and I started in 1997. I'll be up to $10.15 here in about a week. And I think I've really grown; I've had a lot of opportunities, and the benefits [including vacation and health care], I think they're not that bad. I mean they're not the best, but they're there."

Figure 3.6 Differential Effects of Increase to Full-Time Work by Wage Growth Potential on Child Academic Progress, Longer-Run Model Results

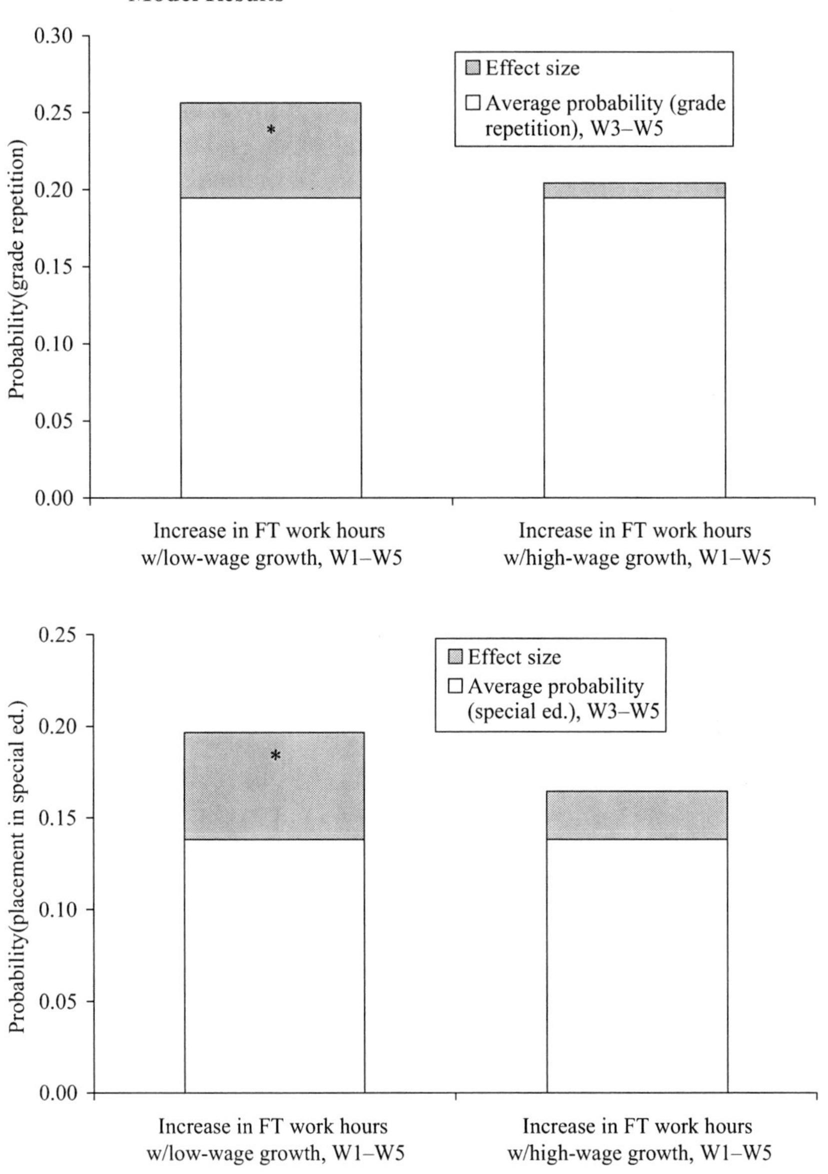

NOTE: *p<0.10.

As a supervisor, Sarah has many responsibilities in addition to customer service. She must track inventory, calculate markdowns on seafood items, place orders and track other items using the computer, manage a small staff, and even unload the delivery trucks once a week. "I'm never standing still," she says, which makes her happy. Her further duties as a union delegate give her the opportunity to stay abreast of the latest news and notices via email and to keep her fellow employees in the loop. In other words, her job is varied, it demands more mentally than a repetitive factory job or a checkout cashier, and there is little of the monotony that can so drain a person. In addition, she has advanced regularly and sees future opportunities for further advancement.

This does not mean everything flows smoothly on the home front. As a single mother of three children, ages 9, 13, and 20, she feels the strain of working full time. She too is disappointed when she has to miss school performances or other activities. And she too worries that her absence might be hurting her children. However, when she describes her children, it quickly becomes apparent that they are involved in many positive activities and that they are thriving in ways that were not always evident among other, less stable mothers Seefeldt interviewed.

"My daughter's got a lot of stuff going on," says Sarah. "She's into this science project—we're so far behind on that, I've got to get that together—and then, like, next week, Saturday, on my day off, I've got to go pick up $700 worth of girl scout cookies and put them in my Blazer. And then this Saturday, because I'm off, I have to work the cookie booth from 1:30 to 4:00 with the girls because the other two coleaders, they have to go to a basketball game. But . . . because there's so much stuff going on in her life, sometimes I can't be at everything, and that kind of upsets me. 'Cause she has a lot of stuff. She's into drama, she's on the dance team, you name it, she's in it. She's in the Youth Advisory Council Board. I keep her busy."

Sarah's steady, full-time work in a job that she enjoys makes juggling family and work, if not easy, at least less stressful than if she dreaded going to work each day. This in turn is evident in her children's success in school and at home. Dance, Girl Scouts, science projects, drama—these are activities that provide role models, structure, and cultivate the habits of success that are evident in our most successful children.

In contrast, Lorraine, a single mother of three, works in housekeeping at a psychiatric unit in a local hospital, earning slightly more than minimum wage for 32 hours a week of backbreaking and menial work of cleaning toilets, mopping hallways, stripping bedding—hardly work that challenges the mind. Lorraine has been on the job for four years now after a string of lower-paying jobs, first in fast food, followed by a short stint as a receptionist, and most recently as a cashier. Her pay raises have been tiny, "just a few nickels and dimes more, that's all." She worries that her children are suffering from the strain that nearly full-time menial work at low wages puts on her—and given our results, she may have cause to worry.

She is contemplating going back to school so she can advance beyond the low-wage, uninspiring jobs she finds herself in, but doing so would require her to be gone even more, with added stress and strain. "I think my kids are hurt from that, and so it's kinda, it's kinda bad either way," she says.

"I've got to support them," Lorraine continues, "but also I got to spend quality time with them too, so and I don't think I can do that balancing two jobs, going back to school, plus being a mom. I think that would be a lot of stress on me, and I don't want that because if I had a lot of stress, then . . . my kids [are] gonna suffer from me stressing, because I'm going to take that stress out on somebody, and it might be my kids and I don't want that."

Even Sarah, with the higher pay and more secure and interesting job, feels the financial strain of low wages, which points to the bind that many of these women face. She currently has difficulty keeping her cupboards stocked, particularly with a 16-year-old son who is "an eating machine." She finds herself meting out proportions to her children to ensure that the food stretches to the end of the month. Earning too much to receive food stamps, she cannot understand how working and playing by the rules ends up hurting her.

"I can remember the time when my kids were younger and I had a part-time job. I mean, I always had a job, I always worked, but the state used to help you out a little bit more. People used to be lazy. They got away with a lot, you know, and I know people still gets away with a lot. But it's just like, see now that I'm working and I'm trying to make ends meet, and I just feel that the state should be there more for people that's out there trying to make things better for themselves, because I could use the food assistance to help me out. I mean, I'm struggling, and I'm being honest, I'm just struggling. I do it, but very thinly. It's really thin."

"Actually," Sarah says, "I lived better off the welfare system than I'm living off my damn paycheck right now . . . I used to call people welfare queens, back in the day . . . And I don't want to be on it now . . . but I would like some food help."

NOT ALL WORK IS DETRIMENTAL

What Olivia, Lorraine, and other single, working-poor mothers have in common in the postwelfare world are the generally low wages, inflexible supervisors, and often unpredictable hours, which means fluctuating paychecks and schedules. The average hourly wage of study participants was $8.28 per hour in 2003, up from $6.83 per hour in 1997. On average, one in five mothers in our study reported that their hours or schedules fluctuated.[4] It is this instability and unpredictability that contributes to their children's behavior problems, as well as work in less mentally demanding jobs.

On the other hand, as some welfare reformers predicted, work can instill routines that were absent, offer mothers a sense of control, and bolster their own sense of self-worth. These outcomes, reformers argued, will trickle down to their children, who will see their mothers heading out to work each day, understanding that to succeed in life requires hard work and sacrifice. The routines may, in turn, order their frequently unsteady lives, and the extra money will offer stability that will benefit everyone.

Caroline, a nurse and single mother of three teens, fits this profile to a tee. Early on as a young mother and high school dropout, Caroline had always wanted to be a nurse, but the prospects seemed dim with three young children.

"I started off as a welfare mother," she says, "a single parent with children, and I can remember when I first started off and said, "I'm going to go back to school, I'm going to be a nurse." And I can remember people saying, 'Yeah right, she ain't going to do nothing.' They kind of knocked me, you know, defeated me before I even started."

Yet with the constant encouragement and support of her own parents, she persevered. She returned to school in the evenings for nursing, and worked part time during the day in a hospital to gain experience. Her mother was a constant presence throughout, providing child care, running children to appointments or to after-school programs. "My mom, she really backed me and helped me out a lot with that. Both my parents really supported me a lot. Now they just support me morally, you know, 'You can do it, whatever you want to do.' That's good, and if I need a ride or the kids need a ride or whatever, if I need somebody to watch the youngest one, my mom's there. If I'm ever in a rut financially, her and my dad are there."

And true to welfare reformers' predictions, Caroline's children have come to appreciate their mother's efforts, and they have absorbed her credo that one must work hard for everything they get. Echoing reformers' words, Caroline says, "It's important to me to be a good role model for them. A part of it was for myself and it made me feel better about myself, but a part of it was to show them anything you believe in, anything you want, you can achieve."

Her daughter recently wrote Caroline a letter that made all the work and sacrifice worth it. "It almost makes me want to cry," she says, "because she was so . . . In the letter, she told me how proud she was of me. She said when people talk about role models, she said, you are my role model because you are so strong and you are there for us."

The key, however, is that the work does not leave families in poverty and that the work is steady, with a sense of predictability that can indeed instill a routine and order in the household. Caroline has worked the same position for eight years, and as of 2004 was earning $19.00 an hour. She works the evening shift from 3:00 p.m. to 11:00 p.m., although she would prefer the first shift so she could spend more time with her family in the evenings. "Right now," she says, "It's like now we're hit and miss. I'm off now, they're at school. When I come home from work, they're in bed." But her children, she says, are getting old enough now that they are independent, and she has a built-in support system in her mother.

She also appreciates the pay, the generous benefits, and the steady schedule. "A bad job," she says, "would be where, if every time you came in either you were forced to work over or you were sent home because you weren't needed. That would be terrible!" Indeed, she is right, given the results we find.

Her steady advancements have left her with a strong sense of self-worth, and she plans to soon return to school for her bachelor's degree, with intentions to move to a high-tier hospital to expand her experience base. "It's all about that self-esteem and that drive," she says of her success. "If you want it bad enough you will achieve it, and I just see so many who don't believe they can achieve it."

Yet she does not for a minute discount the struggle and the strains of single motherhood. Perhaps this is why the results from our study point to the pitfalls of work for single mothers and their children. As even Caroline, one of the most successful of the mothers Seefeldt interviewed, reminds us: "Stress [as a single mother] is day to day because somebody always needs something, somebody always wants something, and then there's always a bill that needs to be paid. The weight lies on my shoulders because I don't have that spouse to say to, 'Well, honey, you know what, I just can't handle this today. You take care of it.' There's nobody but me to take care of it.

"I am so tired. I had to go to a parent conference here, a parent conference at this school, I had to go to the grocery store, rush to Consumer's [Energy], pay the [electricity] bill, pay the water bill, had to get some groceries—oh! I forgot I was supposed to go over here and pick up the clothes at the cleaners. Oops, he told me to pick him up at football practice! It's just that type of day. And when it's just [me], I'm just tired. When is there going to be a day for me?"

As a final way of summarizing our results, we relate mothers' work profiles over the entire study period to child outcomes at the end of the survey. Our three different representative work experience profiles characterize the range of work pattern trajectories among our sample of women and parallel the full spectrum of experiences illuminated in the stories of Olivia, Trudy, Sarah, Caroline, and their children. Roughly one-quarter of women in our sample fit the low-profile work trajectory definition over the study period characterized by chronic instability. On the other end of the spectrum, an equal-sized proportion fit the high-profile work trajectory characterized by upward mobility with employment stability and regular work hours for the vast majority of the period. The remaining one-half of women were somewhere in between these two experiences. Specifically, we use the low-, medium-, and high-profile maternal work patterns experienced over the 1997–2003 period (as defined in Chapter 2) to predict child behavioral outcomes and academic progress indicators at the end of the study. These results are presented in Table 3.7.

For these results, we account for the influence of the relevant initial child outcome measure at wave 1, child age, gender, race, maternal age and education, home literacy, family structure, and living arrangements. Even after accounting for the influence of all those factors, we

Table 3.7 Predicted Child Outcome at End of Study by Mothers' Work Experience Profiles, 1997–2003[a]

	BPI @W5	Externalizing @W5	Internalizing @W5	Prob(grade repetition)
Low profile	0.24**	0.22***	0.33***	0.29*
Medium profile	−0.02	0.03	−0.03	0.26
High profile	−0.19	−0.25	−0.26	0.19

NOTE: *Low profile* defined as not employed in "good" job by wave 5 and had experienced chronic job instability and/or fluctuating work hours for the vast majority of study period (i.e., either had been fired/laid-off two or more times, had experienced four or more voluntary job-to-nonemployment transitions, and/or had two or more years of fluctuating work hours over the seven-year study period). *Medium profile* defined as not employed in "good" job by wave 5, some job instability or fluctuating work hours, but not persistently so to be categorized as low profile, and improvement in work trajectory not great enough to be categorized as high profile. *High profile* defined as employed in "good" job by wave 5 and had experienced employment stability and regular work hours for the vast majority of study period (i.e., had not been fired/laid-off, had experienced three or fewer voluntary job-to-nonemployment transitions, and one or fewer periods of fluctuating work hours over the seven-year study period). *indicates difference in predicted child outcome between low profile and high profile is significant at the 10 percent level. **indicates difference in predicted child outcome between low profile and high profile is significant at the 5 percent level. ***indicates difference in predicted child outcome between low profile and high profile is significant at the 1 percent level.

[a] These models include controls for initial child outcome measure at wave 1, child age, gender, race, maternal age and education, home literacy, family structure, and living arrangements.

find that over the longer run, children whose mothers experienced the low-profile work trajectory during the period had behavior problems at the end of the survey that were roughly half a standard deviation higher than the levels of behavior problems observed among children whose mothers experienced the high-profile work trajectory. Maternal employment patterns are powerful predictors of child outcomes. These results suggest that if a child's mother switched from the low-profile to the high-profile trajectory, it could move children who were originally average down to about the 31st percentile in problem behaviors. Thus, a child whose level of behavior problems exceeded half this low-income population of children would now exhibit fewer behavior problems than 69 percent of the sample of children. Furthermore, 29 percent of children whose mothers experienced the low-profile work trajectory had repeated a grade by the end of the study, compared with 19 percent among children whose mothers experienced the high-profile work trajectory. Well-being among children whose mothers experienced the medium profile fell somewhere in between.

EFFECTS OF OTHER MEASURES

One of the aims of our analysis was to examine whether the effects of a mother's employment on her children's behavior were due to various factors, such as use of child care, her interactions with her children, her physical or mental health, stress, changes in the level and composition of income, or frequent moves from home to home. Although these possibilities were unable to account for the relationships between mothers' work and children's behavior described above, some of the factors had interesting independent effects. Clearly different environments place children at risk for, or insulate them from, developmental problems. We summarize briefly some our findings. The full set of these results is shown in Tables A.1–A.3 in Appendix A.

Our first finding suggests that Sarah might have room to worry, as our results indicate that recent as well as cumulative experiences of food insufficiency and receipt of welfare have detrimental effects on child development. We also find that father involvement in childrearing, parental stress, stressful life events, social support, maternal education, the home literacy environment, harsh parenting, maternal alcohol or drug use problems, and maternal health problems are all significantly related to child behavior problems. The inclusion of all of these factors, however, did not significantly alter the magnitude of the effects of the employment-related variables. For example, the results indicate that increases in parental stress are significantly related to worse internalizing behavior problems. Additionally, mothers who are single or cohabiting (versus married) report higher levels of internalizing behavior problems among their children. We also see that maternal alcohol/drug use and maternal health problems significantly affect child internalizing behavior problems.

One factor of particular note is that of evictions, which we find lead to greater externalizing and internalizing behavior problems (see Figure 3.7). Skyrocketing housing costs over the period were not

Figure 3.7 The Effects of Involuntary Residential Instability on Child Well-Being: Behavior Problems, Child Fixed-Effect Results

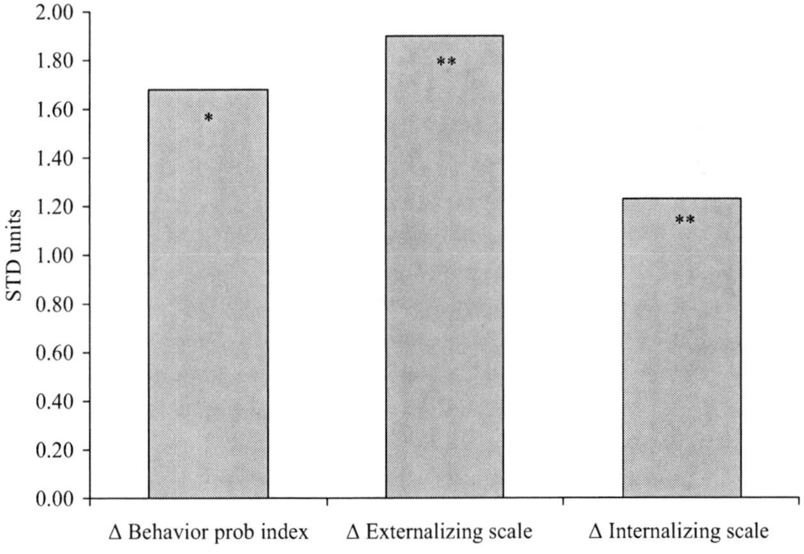

NOTE: **p<0.05; *p<0.10. These results are the estimated effects of eviction in a given year on year-to-year changes in child behavioral outcomes.

matched by increases in housing assistance, raising the risk of eviction or homelessness. Housing prices, which constitute a substantial share of lower-income family budgets, have risen substantially over the past decade in many areas, and the share of budgets going toward housing has increased. Increases in evictions among families with children during economic downturns are one by-product. A significant minority of children in these low-income households experienced housing instability or involuntary relocation that was directly related to their mothers' unstable jobs. About one-fifth of children experienced an eviction over the course of the study.

These findings highlight the precarious economic position of low-income, mostly single mothers in the postwelfare reform era, and they raise important concerns about housing stability and the well-being of children.

Neither evictions nor any of the other variables in the expanded model, however, appeared to explain the associations between unstable work and children's well-being, suggesting that these linkages are due either to unmeasured aspects of mothers' time or perhaps the organization of family time that matter for children's well-being and that are constrained by mothers' extensive or unpredictable work.

RECAP OF MAIN RESULTS

Our study of maternal work after welfare reform and the well-being of children is among the most comprehensive to date on the topic. Our data offered the opportunity to examine numerous aspects of child well-being, including externalizing and internalizing behavior problems, disruptive behavior at school, school absenteeism, grade repetition, and placement in special education. Exploiting the unique features of the WES data, we provide some of the first evidence in the post-1996 welfare reform era on the links between maternal work experiences and longer-run trajectories of child well-being.

Most work on the relationship between maternal employment and child well-being has taken a static view in characterizing employment patterns. These traditional snapshot measures do not provide a meaningful understanding of the dynamic relationships between maternal employment and child well-being. This is the case particularly among low-income families.

Only a handful of prior studies have examined changes over time in child development when mothers leave welfare and begin work. These studies are limited in their ability to inform policy, however, because they have largely ignored the considerable variation in mothers' work experiences after welfare reform. This variation reflects the experiences of mothers with positive trajectories that include stable work, good wages, and upward mobility, but also experiences that are decidedly less positive, including job instability, low wages, and nonstandard work conditions.

The consistency of our results across several models bolsters our confidence in the findings of the consequences of maternal employment for low-income children. We summarize our main findings below.

- Children exhibit fewer behavior problems when mothers work and experience job stability (relative to children whose mothers do not work).
- The type of work matters. How mothers' work experiences influence child behavior outcomes and their academic progress depends on the stability of that work in terms of both hours and job transitions.
- Children whose mothers experienced greater job instability, particularly due to being laid off or fired, have consistently worse behavior problems and academic progress indicators (relative to children whose mothers experienced stable work patterns).
- While a single job loss over the period is associated with a small detrimental impact on child behavior outcomes, these negative effects intensify with multiple occurrences of instability accumulated over time.
- When a mother moves from stable, predictable hours to fluctuating hours, children's behavior problems increase. More time working in jobs with fluctuating hours consistently yields worse child behavior problems (relative to children whose mothers experienced stable work patterns).
- Full-time work has negative longer-run consequences for children only when jobs offer limited wage growth potential. Such

negative consequences do not occur when this work experience requires cognitive skills that lead to higher wage growth prospects and lower turnover in future periods.

- Fluctuating levels of work hours and full-time work in jobs with limited wage growth prospects are strongly associated with probability that the child will repeat a grade or be placed in special education.
- Taken together, these results suggest that "welfare reform," when considered more broadly to include the new landscape of employment for low-income mothers, has imposed some risks to children's development.

Notes

1. We estimate the impact of the cumulative maternal employment experiences between wave 1 and wave 5 on the transition probabilities for these outcomes between the final two waves to ensure that the maternal employment pattern preceded the assessed child outcome.
2. Among national samples of non-college-educated women in the first year of job tenure, prior work has documented a median job duration of nine months, and average annual job mobility (i.e., job-to-job turnover) and job instability (i.e., job-to-nonemployment turnover) rates of 18 percent and 28 percent, respectively (Gladden and Taber 2000; Holzer and LaLonde 2000).
3. There is some noncomparability in the characterization of involuntary job loss (i.e., being fired/laid off) because of changes in the wording of these questions across waves, so we emphasize the involuntary job loss effects in the longer-run models as opposed to the short-run models that use between-wave changes that could instead reflect changes in the wording of the survey question.
4. The shares reporting fluctuating hours or schedules declined from 28 percent at wave 1 to 16 percent by wave 5, for an average of 20 percent across the seven years.

4
Conclusions and Policy Implications

Mary Jo Bane, who resigned from the Clinton administration in response to welfare reform, said in an *American Prospect* article in 1997, "Sadly, there are almost no data to indicate what happens to these families and their children when they are no longer receiving welfare. It is possible to offer some guesses, however. Some of the families are no doubt fine, having found jobs, decent living situations, and adequate child care, so that their children are well cared for and safe. Others are likely to be in situations of great instability, both in their work and in their housing" (p. 52).

We now have evidence that was absent in 1997, and Bane's estimates were surprisingly prescient. It is clear from our findings that the type of job a mother holds and the intensity of her work matters. Simply working, per se, is not necessarily a risk to child behavior and well-being. In fact, working in a stable job benefits children. However, when a mother cannot rely on a regular schedule, when her hours fluctuate from week to week, and when she works full time in a job with limited wage growth and menial tasks, her children's behavior deteriorates. If, however, she works longer hours in a challenging job with real opportunities for a raise, her children's behavior is not affected.

It is not hard to imagine that the adverse effects might be explained, at least in part, by the harried home lives of time-pressed, tired, and stressed mothers, such as Mary Ann, Tamar, Olivia, Lorraine, and the other women we profiled in earlier chapters. The types of jobs they held were often less than stimulating. Working in a factory, cleaning homes, manning the cash register, and doling out food in a soup kitchen are monotonous jobs, typical of the low-wage grind. It is telling, then, that longer work hours have negative consequences for children only when the work offers little potential for wage growth, as is typical of a dead-end job. Also telling, the negative consequences of long work hours are offset when jobs demand more than just showing up, which in turn more often leads to more frequent raises.

Although children are not sleeping on grates and they have not been placed on a forced march to poverty without a safety net, as Daniel Patrick Moynihan and Peter Edelman warned prior to passage of PRWORA, children are not immune to the changes that reform wrought. Their lives have changed dramatically since welfare reform, sometimes for the better, sometimes not. Whereas previously their mothers were home after school, they are now at work, or asleep after working the night shift. Some, like Caroline and her children, are benefiting from the added income, the enhanced self-esteem that stimulating work and advancement brings, and the new order and role models that can positively affect children. Others, however, scramble to find steady child care with neighbors or grandmothers, or whoever else is available at the time to watch over them; unfortunately, this care is seldom stimulating for kids. Mothers like Olivia worry about their children eating poorly or not finishing their homework. Like Sarah, they worry about not being there for them, or missing the important moments in their school lives. They also worry about missing clues that something at school is amiss and being able to intervene early before the problem gets worse.

Unlike the more prestigious positions in the white-collar world, their jobs offer little flexibility to slip out for a few hours in the afternoon to see a dance recital or a band concert or to schedule a teacher conference. Nor is there money to hire a nanny or an au pair to see to it that the children eat well, do their homework, and get fresh air and exercise. And like Tamar, who flopped in the chair exhausted after a day's work and a long commute on a bus, mothers are often bone tired and "ready to snap," as Lorraine says, after a day in a dead-end job.

They are not alone, of course. Married mothers are often in the same boat. Today more than 6 in 10 women with school-age children are in the workforce. The difference for the women in our study and the more privileged women in the workforce is that all-important bottom line: money. Tight budgets make for tough choices, and the lack of money gnaws at a family until often health suffers and tempers flare. Money also allows parents to invest in those extra tutoring classes or the educational toys or books that benefit young children's early development. More fundamental basics also come up short when stretching $20,000 a year to feed three children. As Sarah, working full time at a grocery store at roughly $10 per hour said, "I have to proportion out food a lot more. It just ain't there and it won't last. And that's one of my biggest issues of a single working mom, because, you know, I am out there working. When the kids are little, you can make a little bit of macaroni and cheese or whatever and get away with it, but now [that they are older], it takes a lot of money." Sarah has turned to credit cards to fill gaps in the budget and now is slipping behind on the payments. She faces the choice of selling her home to pay off the bills, "but my house is more important to me," she says. "I have to look at it that way because I have to have a place to live. But it's just life, and I worry every day."

Sarah is not alone in her struggles. Hardship was common among our sample. Lights were turned off, bills piled up, and mothers sometimes went without food. Living on the brink also means that when a car breaks down, there is no money to rent a car for a week while it gets fixed, if the family can afford to fix it at all. As a result, mothers quit their jobs or get fired, and the bills pile up even higher. Turning to credit cards or payday lenders only digs them a deeper hole, and the families soon find themselves packing the boxes to move to a cheaper apartment in a worse neighborhood. And the cycle continues.

As the current economy declines, families up the income ladder begin to experience some of these hardships, and stories of strain and stress, foreclosures, divorce, and debt fill newspaper pages. These are the same strains that mothers in our study faced every day, and have been facing often for decades. Perhaps that is one reason why the previous studies of welfare reform outlined in Chapter 1—the Minnesota, Connecticut, New Hope, and Canadian studies—showed positive results for children of working mothers only when the welfare program supplemented the meager wages with $100 or $200 a month. Without the extra boost of income, mothers, like those in our study, remain perilously close to poverty.

Therefore, the question that Jason DeParle, with whom we began this book, posed in *American Dream* remains: "How much will low-wage work alone change the trajectory of underclass life? What if the mothers' jobs leave them poor? What if they're still stuck in the ghetto? What if their kids still lack fathers?" (p. 113).

The findings presented here are unique in identifying the possible consequences for children of policies designed to promote work among low-income mothers. It is worth recalling that a key goal of welfare reform was to "break the cycle" of poverty and unemployment from one generation to the next. It is only by following the children of former welfare recipients in the postreform era that we can know whether their developmental trajectories point toward a brighter future (economically at least) than the one their own mothers once faced. Our long-run study is uniquely positioned to assess this important component of welfare reform's original goals.

In addition to providing insights into the intergenerational consequences of welfare reform, we hope our findings will inform policy. Ours is one of the first studies to assess the consequences for children of the considerable variation in mothers' work experiences after welfare reform. As we now know, this variation includes positive job experiences, including stable work, good wages, and upward mobility, but it also includes decidedly less positive experiences, including job instability, low wages, and nonstandard work schedules. We have identified children who may be at risk because of these employment challenges. We hope these findings not only assist policymakers and practitioners in better understanding the consequences of welfare reform, but also point to areas in which new policies and supports can be developed.

Ours is among the most comprehensive examinations of life after welfare and its effects on children. The consistency of our results across the many empirical approaches bolsters our confidence in the findings. Importantly, we did not take a static view of the relationship between maternal employment and child well-being. Indeed, if we are to better inform policy, we must examine child development as it changes *over time*, to better capture the often significant variation in mothers' work experiences since welfare reform.

REMAINING PUZZLES

An issue our analysis could not pin down was which factors account for the links between mothers' job experiences and children's behavior problems. In part, this was a function of limitations in our data. Despite including a wide range of potential mediating variables—

such as income levels and its sources, material hardship measures, child care use, residential location changes, parental stress, social support, parenting style, maternal mental and physical health—none explained to a large degree these links. That these other factors were unable to fully or even largely explain the links between a mother's employment and her child's behavior suggests that something else is going on. One possibility is how a mother organizes family time, or how her children spend their time, both of which are affected by extensive, unstable, or unpredictable work.

Although the variables in our study could not explain the links, they were related in expectable ways to our outcomes. As Bane presaged, evictions and a nomadic series of moves from home to home all played a role in the negative child outcomes. These moves, as we showed, were typically precipitated by job losses. With evictions included in the model, the associations between mothers' job loss and children's behavior problems were reduced by about 15 percent, meaning that evictions explained 15 percent of the association. The phenomenon of involuntary moves has received little attention in research devoted to welfare reform and child well-being and deserves greater study in future work in light of the current housing crisis.

Neither evictions nor any of the other variables in the model, however, fully explained the associations between maternal full-time and irregular work and children's emotional well-being, suggesting that these links, as noted, are due to unmeasured aspects of mothers' time or perhaps the organization of family time that matter for children's well-being and that are under pressure by mothers' extensive or unpredictable work.

Future work in this area would be greatly enhanced if we better understood the regularity and quality of family routines and time together. Consistent and predictable routines provide regular opportunities for family members to spend time together, promote family organization and parenting competence, and help children learn to regulate their behavior. Activities as seemingly simple as eating a family meal together, or, say, following a special family ritual every Saturday afternoon, are linked with better school performance and higher emotional well-being in children (Fiese et al. 2002). Mothers in the low-wage workforce often have difficulty in creating and maintaining such family routines when work schedules fluctuate, work hours and commute times are excessive, and unexpected illnesses and emergencies occur. These kinds of work conditions can lead to family members eating at different times of day to accommodate hectic schedules (Devine et al. 2006), or to parents adjusting children's routines to match their own evening and night work schedules (Roy, Tubbs, and Burton 2004; Weisner et al. 2002). Over time, it would not be surprising if constant instability in family routines took its toll on children's emotional health or academic progress.

Our data could also not identify in detail the settings in which children spend time while mothers are working. As we have described, when mothers work, younger children typically spend time in child care. Such care can be in home settings with relatives or other caregivers, or ideally (from the perspective of low-income children's cognitive development) in more organized, center-based settings. On the one hand, nonstandard or irregular hours may mean less time in child care because such schedules may allow mothers to be at home during the daytime hours. On the other hand, mothers in these types of work arrangements often need to sleep during their "time" with children (Newman 2000).

It is likely that the mothers in our study relied on complex and ever-shifting "packages" of child care for their young children (Henly and Lambert 2005). Sarah, the mother working full time in the grocery store, admitted that child care for her nine-year-old, for example, was often catch as catch can. "Like in the summertime, especially, she's at this house, that house, this house, so I get everybody watching her. So I don't have no problem, like, who's got her, you know, she's got somewhere to go. And I don't have to pay nobody to just, like, they go someplace, you know, and I give her a few bucks to go, like if they're going to go skating or to a movie or something like that. But, they feed her, you know, she don't eat much," she laughs.

If the women in our study are similar to other low-income mothers (and we have many reasons to suspect they are), then sometimes their children will be in center-based arrangements, but the package of care they cobble together will almost always include multiple informal care arrangements with relatives and neighbors. Low-wage working mothers typically rely heavily on their own mothers and sisters (and sometimes children's fathers) to provide care for their children; adults in these households often try to work alternating shifts with one another (Newman 2000). Managing and maintaining these various care arrangements can be exhausting and stressful and may result in less than optimal care for children. These types of care arrangements are also vulnerable to changes in work schedules, illness, and changes in adult relationships. Indeed, welfare reform is likely to have made kinship care more difficult to use because grandmothers, sisters, and other women in low-income neighborhoods are more likely to be employed themselves than in years past. Again, it would not be surprising if the constant stress and uncertainty of having to patch together child care arrangements in the face of erratic work schedules and job instability took an emotional toll on the mothers and children in our study. Child care instability, along with job and residential instability, may be one more facet of the instability that characterizes family life in the post–welfare reform era.

We also know less than we wish we did about how older children in our study were cared for. Lorraine's son Marcus skirted several attempts by boys in his high school to co-opt him to sell drugs. Luckily for Lorraine, as she readily admits, Marcus now holes up in his room most days, listening to music. Sarah's 16-year-old son is "off on his own" after school. And Tamar's son, unfortunately, ended up in the juvenile justice system after drifting away from school. Although older children typically still require some level of care and supervision during nonschool hours, this may happen in a wider range of settings than for younger children. In addition to formal afterschool programs and home-based care, school-age children can be involved in a variety of more- and less-structured activities—from participating in organized team sports or school clubs, to spending time with friends at a community center. Some antipoverty programs have had positive effects on children's academic performance and social behavior by increasing children's participation in structured out-of-school activities (Huston et al. 2001). Such structured opportunities might be important not only for the adult supervision that they provide to children but also because of the regularity or stability of the routine itself, and perhaps too the opportunity for children to form positive emotional bonds with adult caregivers, mentors, and coaches.

Issues of monitoring are also more salient for the older children in our study, but we did not have a good measure of this important dimension of parenting in our survey. More extensive monitoring may be required in low-income, inner-city neighborhoods, where risky influences, like those Marcus and Tamar's son Omar faced in high school, are more prevalent. If a mother is working nonstandard or erratic hours, her children risk spending more time unsupervised, with potentially negative consequences, particularly if this time is spent only with peers (Lopoo 2007; Pettit et al. 1997). It is not surprising that unsupervised time has been found to be especially risky for children living in low-income or dangerous neighborhoods (Smolensky and Gootman 2003).

In summary, despite testing a wide range of potential mediating factors, none was sufficient to fully, or even largely, explain the outcomes. That is not to say they played no role. But they alone were not the only reasons for the impact on behavior. The overall inability of our many mediating variables to explain the links between employment and child behavior point to other aspects of mothers' time, the organization of family time, or children's own time use that matter for children's well-being and that are constrained by mothers' extensive, unstable, or unpredictable work. More research is clearly warranted to unpack these effects more carefully.

ANTICIPATING THE FUTURE

In thinking about the meaning of our results, a key question concerns the longer-run impacts on the child behavior. Recall that in this sample of low-income children, the rates of externalizing behavior problems (e.g., acting-out behavior, problems with self-control) were significantly higher than in national samples. This corresponds to research showing that low-income children are in worse health (broadly defined to include physical and emotional health) than their higher-income peers (Currie and Lin 2007). In national data, mental health problems are both more common and more limiting in low-income populations than in higher-income groups. Moreover, problems with self-control and other dimensions of emotion regulation are the key factors (aside from ability) that teachers rate as critical for learning (Blair 2002).

One can imagine, then, that elevated rates of behavior problems in early childhood portend greater problems down the road. Recent work by economists, using large-scale representative data and sophisticated analytic methods, illustrates these very associations (Currie and Stabile 2006). Results from such studies show that children's mental health and behavior problems significantly lower future test scores and school attainment, in both high- and low-income populations. Unfortunately, our data do not allow us to simulate the likelihood of specific poor outcomes for children in later life because we lack diagnostic criteria for conditions such as ADHD and the like. Nevertheless, well-controlled longitudinal studies show significant connections between general indices of behavior problems among school-age children and their future educational outcomes, earnings, and probabilities of employment (Currie and Stabile 2006). These studies also show that the relationship between behavior problems and poor academic achievement is a linear one. In other words, even children with minor behavior problems (such that they would never receive a diagnosis) may nevertheless fare more poorly than their peers who do not exhibit any behavior problems at all.

PROMISING OPTIONS—IMPROVING JOB RETENTION AND ADVANCEMENT FOR LOW-INCOME WORKING PARENTS

What then, would it take to improve the employment experiences, behavioral outcomes, and academic progress of the children of low-income women like the ones in our sample? Unfortunately there are no easy policy solutions, and supportive evidence for the seemingly most promising interventions is not yet available. Although recognizing there is no "magic bullet," we describe some promising models that, although not yet fully evaluated, warrant more attention.

The results from our study suggest that policies that improve job retention and increase advancement for low-income working parents could have substantively important effects—not only for their obvious economic benefits, but also for reducing behavior problems and improving academic outcomes among children. Increased employment stability could potentially also be achieved by helping mothers find work at jobs with more regular and predictable schedules.

Here, we discuss several promising approaches, including those that intervene on the labor market side of the low-wage job market, as well as those that would intervene directly with workers themselves.

Enhancing Stability of Work Schedules

Nationally, we do not know how many workers have unpredictable schedules. However, as our data reveal, this phenomenon is widespread: between 20 and 30 percent of the women in our study worked at a job characterized by fluctuating hours at any given survey wave. These unpredictable scheduling practices are a typical employer strategy for managing fluctuations in consumer demand (Henly and Lambert 2005). Work schedules in many retail environments are typically set with notices of one week or less, with frequent last-minute changes to posted schedules (Henly, Shaefer, and Waxman 2006). As well, workers' ability to exert control over these scheduling practices is haphazard and often depends on the idiosyncrasies of personal relationships with their supervisors. As we have described previously, unpredictable schedules can interfere with workers' ability to effectively structure and use nonwork hours, making it difficult to plan family meals, adopt consistent homework and bedtime routines, participate in children's school activities, and maintain consistent child care arrangements (Henly, Shaefer, and Waxman 2006).

Lambert and Henly have developed a promising intervention, the "Scheduling Intervention Study," with hourly workers in the Chicago area (Lambert 2009). The intervention is assessing the effects of greater schedule predictability (i.e., posting schedules further in advance) and improved communication (between employees and employers on issues related to scheduling) on workers' performance, daily family practices, health, and well-being. This unique program has only recently been implemented and as such does not have impacts to guide specific policy development.

Improving Women's Ability to Keep the Jobs They Get

Our study shows that job instability is common among mothers. Therefore, another key policy question centers on how we can improve the chances that women will keep their jobs, and thereby help reduce their children's behavior problems and poor academic outcomes.

The federally funded Employment Retention and Advancement (ERA) evaluation, the largest and most comprehensive random assignment evaluation of its kind, was initiated in 1998 and aims to test a variety of strategies, through 18 program tests in eight different states, for promoting retention and job advancement for working welfare recipients and other low-wage workers.[1] The programs target advancement for working welfare recipients by encouraging and supporting education and training and finding better job "matches." Programs also try to improve job placement and retention for those at risk of losing a job due to physical or mental health problems, substance problems, or long-term welfare dependency. Many challenges to implementing these programs have been noted, in large part because program staff lacked existing models to replicate.

Although program impacts from the full set of interventions have not yet been published (nor has the planned cost-benefit analysis), some of the early results are, unfortunately, somewhat discouraging.[2] Several of the programs were never fully implemented and, not surprisingly, had no effects on employment, earnings, or receipt of public assistance. In California, results from the Los Angeles site found that unemployed welfare recipients in an enhanced job club had no better employment outcomes than participants in a traditional job club. In Riverside, California, two of the education and training programs had small impacts on attendance in basic education or training; however, neither program increased employment and earnings levels for participants over two years. In Minnesota, which adopted a case management program for long-term welfare recipients, the program showed little effect on participants' involvement in program services or on their employment, earnings, or public assistance receipt during the first one-and-a-half years of follow-up. The Texas program, which emphasized a mix of job placement, retention, and advancement, showed small and inconsistent effects on employment and retention outcomes during the first two years of follow-up. Similarly, in South Carolina, the program had little effect on employment rates, earnings, employment retention, or advancement.

One exception to this sobering pattern was in New York City's Personal Roads to Individual Development and Employment (PRIDE) program, which was designed to improve job retention and advancement for welfare recipients with work-limiting medical and mental health conditions. The results from PRIDE were somewhat more encouraging in that participants had increased employment and decreased welfare payments. At the same time, about two-thirds of the PRIDE group never worked during the two-year period, and many were sanctioned, which raises important questions about the types of interventions that need to be developed for a group of welfare recipients with these kinds of barriers to employment.

Indeed, we think it is imperative to understand and address the elevated rates of mental and physical health problems, including depression, that characterize the respondents in the WES and participants in many other studies of low-income women (Danziger et al. 2000). Case management and service provision may be particularly important when dealing with these problems, but clearly it will not be an easy task to design just one program that addresses the myriad psychosocial problems faced by many low-income parents. That said, efforts to develop such programs must continue because mental and physical health problems are substantively important in predicting low-income women's reliance on public assistance and their ability to get and keep jobs, over and above their cognitive abilities (Kunz and Kalil 1999). For instance, in other analyses with the WES data, Sandra Danziger and colleagues showed that after controlling for welfare recipients' work experience, education, and job skills (i.e., their "cognitive skills"), as well as measures of their drug use and physical health problems, those recipients with major depression were 9 percentage points less likely to be working than similar women who were not depressed. By way of comparison, those who lacked a high school degree were 12 percentage points less likely to be working than similar women with a high school degree (Danziger et al. 2000).

Moreover, in a comprehensive summary of experimental welfare to work programs by Charles Michalopolous and colleagues, the one exception to the overall positive intervention impacts on earnings was when participants were at risk of depression. That is, the demonstration programs did not affect earnings for those at high risk of depression when they entered the study, and the programs had smaller effects on earnings for those at high risk versus low risk of depression (Michalopoulos, Schwartz, and Adams-Ciardullo 2001). The smaller impact on depressed mothers' earnings might stem from participants' slower movement into the workforce (that is, less ability to get jobs), but it could also stem from these women's greater risk of losing the jobs they had (that is, greater job instability).

In our own study, mothers who experienced job instability (compared with those who experienced employment stability) were less educated. Perhaps not surprisingly, given their frequent job losses, they also had lower earnings and hence lower family income and a greater likelihood of welfare receipt during the study period. And, as we have described, they were more likely to have been evicted, perhaps because they lacked sufficient income to pay the rent, particularly after a job loss. But in addition, they were more likely to have problems with drugs and alcohol, to have a physical health problem, and to be depressed. Earlier in this monograph, we noted the very high rates of maternal depression and other psychiatric disorders such as posttraumatic stress disorder among the mothers in the WES. We cannot say for certain whether these mothers' physical and psychosocial health problems are the cause or a consequence of their job instability; the associations probably run in both directions. However, this portrait of a multiplicity of problems resonates with a group that social policy researchers have recently focused on: those "hard to employ" individuals who face barriers to employment that go beyond limited education or a lack of work experience (Bloom et al. 2007).

It is critical that we learn what types of interventions can be developed for those who suffer from a variety of such barriers to employment, and the specific ways in which such problems affect finding and keeping jobs. In one promising intervention, the Rhode Island "Working Toward Wellness" Project, which was implemented in late 2006, the target population is working-age parents who are on Medicaid and have undiagnosed depression. An enhanced treatment group receives intensive telephone outreach and follow-up from managed care case managers to encourage participation in mental health treatment. The program provides access to employment services as well (Bloom et al. 2007). The design of this intervention is based on prior random assignment evidence that identified a variety of effective treatments for depression and found also that treatment for depression can reduce job loss (although these impacts have not been identified in an exclusively low-income population). It is also possible that reducing depression in low-income individuals can indirectly benefit children, given the known association between parental depression and children's behavior problems. Although promising, evidence of impacts from this intervention is not yet available.

Improving Low-Income Women's Wage Growth Prospects

Finally, as we saw in our data, toiling away for long hours at a job that offers few prospects for wage growth was associated with poor developmental outcomes for children. How can we increase the likelihood that women can move up the job ladder to higher-skill work that eventually leads to better wages? Having more education or possessing key skills (such as math or literacy) are prime predictors of getting (or moving into) better jobs. However, 35 percent of low-wage workers nationally in low-income families have only a high school degree, and 28 percent lack even that. In contrast, 60 percent of all workers nationally have some postsecondary education.[3] Improving education and skill building in disadvantaged populations, while clearly a worthy goal, is nevertheless a vast undertaking that could begin at birth and might involve targeting numerous dimensions of mothers' development.

Most discussions of skill building or human capital development begin with the idea of increasing education. The National Evaluation of Welfare to Work Strategies (NEWWS), which included an education-focused intervention, was modestly successful (on the order of 8 percentage points) in increasing degree receipt among women who lacked a high school degree at the beginning of the study. Moreover, a reanalysis of the NEWWS data suggests that the education treatment was even more effective among sample members with a stronger, rather than a weaker, sense of "self-efficacy" (that is, the notion that one has the capacity to change important things in one's life) (Leininger and Kalil

2008). These findings highlight the important role of "noncognitive skills," a broad term that often refers to dimensions of mothers' mental health, self-esteem, or sense of self-efficacy (Cunha and Heckman 2008). Results such as this underscore the notion that human capital interventions can be successful even in very disadvantaged populations, particularly among respondents with certain cognitive and noncognitive skills (the NEWWS program was also vastly more effective in increasing educational attainment for women with stronger literacy and numeracy skills at the outset of the program).

In addition, education or training programs will likely be more effective if they focus on ensuring that low-wage workers earn the credentials that employers value (Holzer and Martinson 2008). Encouraging training programs to align with the demands of the local labor market can also help create better matches between employers and workers, thus increasing workers' wage growth prospects.

Addressing job retention, as discussed above, may also have positive impacts on low-wage workers' wages. Frequent job-to-nonemployment transitions (whether voluntary or involuntary) cause workers to lose seniority and impede work experience and skills that are associated with wage growth (Holzer and Martinson 2008). That said, it would be counterproductive to focus on job retention alone, because being stuck in a low-wage job with few prospects for advancement offers little hope to low-income working parents either. In other words, low-wage workers will benefit from strategies that help them retain good jobs and identify opportunities to move to a better job.

BEYOND INTERVENTION: STRENGTHENING THE SAFETY NET

Beyond these potentially promising interventions to improve employment stability and advancement prospects of low-wage working parents, we believe it is the responsibility of government to provide a set of supports for low-income parents who are "playing by the rules" and working double-duty to earn a living and raise their children, often without the support of a spouse. It is not at all uncommon, as we have seen in the research presented in this monograph, for these workers to encounter hard times in the labor market. Workers are fired, often when their health, mental health, or child care problems interfere with their ability to be good workers. Macroeconomic shifts in demand, such as in the current recession, can also precipitate widespread layoffs, business closings, and rising unemployment.

In such challenging economic times, many families are falling through the cracks of an inadequate safety net. But with a more effective and expanded safety net, children in low-income working families would not have to suffer the material hardship and instability wrought by these forces. Building a policy and research agenda that seeks to bolster the economic security of low-income working families with children must include as priorities increasing the availability of jobs that pay enough so families can make ends meet, increasing the flexibility for parents to balance work and family obligations, increasing accessibility of insurance coverage against the risk of unemployment, affordable and safe housing, health insurance, and stable child care. Public policy may need to play a larger role in managing the risks of a health crisis or a job loss, so that unanticipated events (such as a sick family member or absent child care provider) do not trigger the loss of a job and the onset of deeper economic hardship.

In the post-1996 era, although work pays more than welfare, work alone for a substantial share of single mothers with children is not paying enough to consistently afford the basics—housing, health care, food, and child care—not enough to be prepared for emergencies, and not enough to lay down a path toward long-term economic self-sufficiency. With family income more dependent upon success in the labor market, parental employment circumstances and children's living arrangements are more vulnerable to economic fluctuations (as welfare participation is no longer countercyclical in the post-PRWORA era). Welfare reform may have weakened the social insurance role of public assistance in smoothing consumption patterns in response to negative employment- and family-related changes experienced by low-income families with children. Policies emphasizing work as a means of moving families out of poverty were originally implemented when jobs were plentiful—now, they must operate in a weaker economy when workers with low skills have more limited employment prospects.

Whether work requirements that attempt to rapidly move welfare recipients into employment have greater or smaller long-run effects than programs that attempt some form of increased investment in education and training may well hinge critically on the macroeconomic demand conditions that prevail (Hotz, Imbens, and Klerman 2006).[4] The lessons that can be drawn from the diversity of work experience witnessed in our sample over the study suggest that the best approach is neither a rapid-employment nor an education/training first emphasis for everyone. Rather, a more nuanced approach is needed that separates the caseload according to their needs, requiring rapid-employment for those with significant preexisting job skills and an education and training strategy for those with greater needs for skill improvement and during times of sluggish labor market demand.[5]

Government investments in training and workforce development have dropped by 70 percent in real terms over the past two decades, and the United States ranks among the lowest in spending on "active labor market policy" of industrialized countries (Heckman, Lalonde, and Smith 1999; O'Leary, Straits, and Wandner 2004). In addition to traditional work supports, our evidence suggests the need for increased support of non-employment-related services to address the health, mental health, and family and child concerns of this population.

Housing policy assistance is one example of a route that could be taken to strengthen the safety net for these low-income families. Consider evictions: a clear link in our results is the one between job instability and children's behavior problems, in part through job loss's impact on evictions. Families in our study who experienced job instability also had lower earnings and less household income. Undoubtedly, involuntary job losses can lead to a downward spiral in family's economic resources; a string of missed rent payments can add up and eventually lead to the evictions that we know to be associated with children's behavior problems. In this case, a policy option might be to enhance the availability of short-term emergency financial resources for low-income parents, which would allow them to hold onto their home or apartment during a period of unemployment after being laid off or fired. This is especially important given that the overwhelming majority of families in our sample are "asset poor," lacking enough liquid savings to live for three months at the federal poverty level without earnings.

Of course we would need to be mindful of the costs and benefits associated with such a program, and potentially difficult decisions about eligibility for such a benefit would have to be made, particularly in an era when job and housing losses reach far into the middle class. Yet in the absence of effective programs that promote job stability and advancement among low-income mothers, we can expect the kinds of adverse labor market experiences we have identified here to persist, particularly as we enter into a deepening recession. The present generation of low-income children will continue to be affected by their parents' employment problems. Keeping mothers and children in their homes could go a long way toward stabilizing children's lives, both today and into the future. Doing so would likely also have positive spillovers on mothers' chances of finding a new job.

Another policy route toward stabilizing family income and strengthening the safety net for low-income mothers and children is to reform the Unemployment Insurance (UI) System. The overwhelming majority of women in our study who lose jobs are ineligible for UI benefits because their jobs have not lasted long enough or they have not worked enough hours. One possibility for overhauling UI eligibility rules is to switch from total wages earned to time worked in order to estimate workers' UI benefit eligibility. Doing so is important because recent evidence has shown that although UI plays a relatively small role in reducing poverty and slowing the rise of poverty during labor market downturns, it is an effective antipoverty tool for the poor who do receive it (Holzer and Martinson 2008). The efficacy of UI as a tool to fight poverty and economic instability among low-income families with children during labor market downturns can be improved by expanding the eligibility of workers from low-income households. Leading policy scholars are now advocating nationwide UI eligibility changes to ensure that low-wage workers are not shut out of the insurance program because of short job tenure, the need to seek part-time work, or failure to meet the minimum earnings requirement (Zedlewski, Holcomb, and Loprest 2007). Many struggling families would be helped if workers who quit their jobs because of illness, pregnancy, family emergency, or domestic violence could still get benefits.

Reforms to the UI system or related programs that provide temporary assistance to job losers can create a more reliable safety net for these workers and stabilize their incomes as they search for new work with better long-term prospects for themselves and their families. Hopefully, major family disruptions for children may thus be avoided. In addition to temporarily extending UI benefits for the long-term unemployed in the current recession, extended UI benefits could include making special funds available to those willing to pursue additional training to build their skills for the next job. This may be particularly important in a period of economic contraction.

Finally, the United States has the dubious distinction of standing out from its peer countries in not providing paid time off that parents can use to care for sick children or take them to doctors' appointments, recover from their own illness, or attend to other personal or family needs (Waldfogel 2009). In the absence of paid and job-protected leave, parents who need to take time off to meet pressing family needs may have their pay docked or lose their job. As the story of Olivia (described in Chapter 3) illustrated, low-income workers' frequent inability to get even a modicum of flexibility in their jobs to respond to unexpected family emergencies compounds frustrations at work and at home. California was the first state to pass paid family leave; their legislation was enacted in 2002 and came into effect in 2004. Among other things, parental leave has been shown to improve maternal health and child health and development as well as increase employment continuity among mothers (Chatterji and Markowitz 2005). In the context of today's living arrangements, with few children having the luxury of a stay-at-home parent, providing some minimal amount of paid and job-protected sick leave should be an important component of antipoverty policy.

Rigorous evaluation research on new program initiatives is still needed for us to be confident about "best practices" and the most effective program designs. When designed effectively, work-family policies can help parents stay in employment more continuously and work more hours, thus leading to higher earnings in the short term and to better earnings growth in the future. Ultimately, children's development will benefit. While new program initiatives may be costly, interventions cannot be postponed without risking the future for today's low-income children. Programs to help ensure the employment stability of less-skilled workers with children can avert the risk of social problems that result from a lack of jobs or inadequate incomes, including crime, underground economic activity, lack of residential stability, and a cycle of poverty and low skills that get passed from one generation to the next. It bears repeating that one of the key goals of welfare reform was to break the cycle of poverty and hardship from one generation to the next. By bolstering the safety net under these economically vulnerable working parents, in concert with implementing a set of well-conceived interventions, we may be able to achieve that goal.

Notes

1. An overview of the ERA can be found on the Web site of the U.S. Department of Health and Human Services, Administration for Children and Families, Office of Planning, Research, and Evaluation: http://www.acf.hhs.gov/programs/opre/welfare_employ/employ_retention/employ_reten_overview.html.
2. A complete set of program reports, along with several reports on implementation and interim findings, can be found on the Web site of the U.S. Department of Health and Human Services, Administration for Children and Families, Office of Planning, Research, and Evaluation: http://www.acf.hhs.gov/programs/opre/welfare_employ/employ_retention/index.html#reports.
3. Greg Acs, Testimony before the Subcommittee on Income Security and Family Support of the House Committee on Ways and Means, September 11, 2008. http://waysandmeans.house.gov/media/pdf/110/acs.pdf (accessed April 15, 2009).
4. Hotz, Imbens, and Klerman (2006) show evidence that greater employment gains are experienced in the longer run for human-capital approaches relative to the work-first approach.
5. Similar arguments have been advocated previously by Dan Bloom and Charles Michalopoulos.

Appendix A
Measures

CHILD OUTCOME MEASURES

The WES survey contains a subset of items from the Behavioral Problems Index (BPI) described in Chase-Lansdale et al. (1991). Unfortunately, the WES did not include the entire 28-item BPI at each wave. The items in these scales ask the mother to report on the child's behavior as she has observed it over the past three months. Mothers respond whether these behaviors are not true, sometimes true, or often true for their child.

The ***externalizing behavior*** scale (three items) includes items such as "bullies or is cruel or mean to others" and "breaks things deliberately." This variable ranges from 3 to 9. Alphas at the first and fifth waves, respectively, are 0.48 and 0.65.

The ***internalizing behavior*** scale (five items) focuses on sadness ("unhappy, sad"), being withdrawn, and feelings ("feels worthless"). Values range from 5 to 15, and the alphas are 0.66 and 0.75 for waves 1 and 5, respectively. These alphas are consistent with those found in the National Longitudinal Survey of Youth (Baker et al. 1993), which also administered the BPI.

Our measure of ***total behavior problems*** is a 12-item summary index that combines these two scales and includes four additional items measuring fear/anxiety in the child.

Disruptive behavior in school is coded 1 if the mother reports that the child is sometimes or often either disobedient in school or has trouble getting along with teachers; 0 otherwise.

School absenteeism problems are coded 1 if the child regularly missed school at least one or more times a month; 0 otherwise.

Repeated a grade or placed in special education is coded 1 if either event occurred since last survey.

CUMULATIVE MEASURES OF MOTHERS' WORK EXPERIENCES

We utilize information on mothers' job tenure, monthly job/employment history, and information collected from self-reported reasons for job changes to characterize employment patterns and the extent of job stability and job mobility over the seven-year study period (February 1997–2004). Using retrospective questions from each wave, we construct cumulative full- and part-time work experience measures that capture the total number of years of work experience accumulated (as of the relevant wave), and the cumulative number of years in which the mother experienced job stability, voluntary job mobility, and job instability. We use the same job transition pattern definitions as discussed in Chapter 2, but summed over the successive periods since February 1997, when respondents were originally observed on the welfare rolls. We also count the total number of years in which the mother experienced fluctuating work hours on the job. These cumulative employment pattern measures are used in the baseline OLS regression models reported in Table 3.4.

FAMILY CHARACTERISTICS USED IN THE FULL MODEL

Used paid child care services is coded 1 if yes since last survey.

Family-income-to-needs ratio is the monthly income-to-needs ratio net of taxes, CPI-U deflated to 1997 dollars.

Maternal earnings is measured at the monthly level and CPI-U deflated to 1997 dollars. In the regressions, this is expressed in thousands of dollars to ease interpretation of effect sizes.

Received welfare is coded 1 if respondent received any income from FIP/TANF in past month.

Food insufficiency is coded 1 if respondent answers sometimes or often not enough to eat to the following question: "Which of the following best describes the amount of food your household has to eat: enough to eat, sometimes not enough to eat, or often not enough to eat?

Moved is coded 1 for yes if the respondent reported moving since the previous survey and/or the residential address changed since the previous survey wave.

Evicted is coded 1 for yes if respondent reports being evicted or experiencing an episode of homelessness since the previous interview.

Neighborhood problems is a summary scale based on 11 self-report items (each item ranges from 1 to 3, with higher scores indicating higher levels of problems) asking the respondent how big a problem the following issues are in her neighborhood: availability of public transportation, availability of affordable housing, slow/no police response, groups of teenagers hanging about, vandalism, prostitution, sexual assault/rape, muggings, gangs, drug use/dealing, and general safety of neighborhood.

Neighborhood poverty rate is the proportion of households in poverty in the census tract in which the family lives.

Parental stress index is a seven-item index that measures the degree of stress or irritation mothers perceive in their interactions with their children. This scale explores mothers' subjective sense of difficulty in the parenting role and, in previous research, has been related to child maltreatment. Items for this scale were taken from or adapted from Abidin's Parenting Stress Index (PSI) (Abidin 1990) and from the New Chance Study (Zaslow and Eldred 1998). A sample item is, "I find that being a mother is much more work than pleasure." Items are measured on a 5-point scale and are coded such that a score of 1 means "never" and a score of 5 means "almost always." The range of the scale is 7–35. Higher scores indicate greater parenting stress. Cronbach's alpha for this scale is 0.81.

Stressful life events index is a summary checklist of seven yes/no items that may have occurred to respondents in the past 12 months, including whether 1) the respondent or one of her children had been robbed or attacked, 2) the respondent had a relative or close friend in jail, 3) she had people living with her that she wished weren't there, 4) a close relation or friend had died or been killed, 5) a close relation or friend had a drug or alcohol problem, 6) she had trouble finding a place to live, and 7) she had been hassled by bill collectors or agencies.

Social support index is a summary checklist of five items (coded 1 if yes) that asks the respondent whether there is someone she could count on to 1) run errands, 2) lend money, 3) give encouragement and reassurance, 4) watch her children, or 5) give her a ride or lend a car if necessary.

Harsh parenting toward the focal child is measured with an eight-item index. Mothers respond "often" (1), "sometimes" (2), or "never" (3) when asked how often they use harsh measures to punish the target child, including spanking, yelling, threatening to send the child away, or talking things over with the child (reverse-coded). A higher score indicates increased use of harsh parenting. Cronbach's alpha for this scale is 0.57. These items were derived from the New Hope Study.

Mothers' alcohol or drug problem is measured by whether the respondent met the diagnostic screening behavior within the 12 months prior to the interview. The screening criteria are derived from the Composite International Diagnostic Interview (CIDI) used in the National Co-Morbidity Study (NCS) and are based on symptoms and conditions specified by the American Psychiatric Association's Diagnostic and Statistical Manual of Mental Disorders (DSM-IV). The respondent received a 1 on this variable if she was alcohol dependent, used drugs, or both. Alcohol dependence is coded affirmatively when a respondent meets any three of the following criteria during a 12-month period: 1) increased tolerance for alcohol; 2) symptoms of withdrawal; 3) increased intake over longer periods of time; 4) persistent desire and/or unsuccessful attempt to curb or control use; 5) spending a lot of time obtaining the substance; 6) reducing number/amount of time in social, occupational, or recreational activities because of use of the substance; or 7) the substance use is continued despite knowledge of having a persistent or recurrent physical or psychological problem that is likely to have been caused or exacerbated by the substance.

The drug use variable equals 1 if the respondent responds affirmatively to the question, "Did you ever use any of the (following) drugs on your own during the past 12 months?" Drug use is indicated if the mother either used illegal drugs in the past 12 months or used prescription drugs to get high in the past 12 months.

Mothers' physical health problem is measured with self-reports of general well-being and the presence of a physical impairment or limitation. Using indicators in the SF-36 Health survey, we define a woman as having health problems if she both self-reports fair or poor health (as opposed to excellent, very good, or good) and if she is in the lowest age-specific quartile of a physical functioning scale (where she rates any limitations in walking, climbing, lifting, carrying, etc.) (Ware, Snow, and Kosinski 1993). Because having only one of these problems may indicate a temporary condition or less severe problem, we count her as health impaired only if she has both.

Mothers' probable diagnosis major depression is measured by whether the respondent met the diagnostic screening behavior for major depression within the 12 months prior to the interview. The screening criteria are derived from the Composite International Diagnostic Interview (CIDI) used in the National Co-Morbidity Study (NCS) and are based upon symptoms and conditions specified by the American Psychiatric Association's Diagnostic and Statistical Manual of Mental Disorders (DSM-IV). To meet the screening criteria for major depression, a respondent has to report a certain number of symptoms and level of impairment in functioning such that a psychiatrist would recommend further clinical assessment. The respondent is asked whether in the past 12 months she felt sad or blue or depressed, or whether she lost interest in things, felt down on herself or worthless or had thoughts of death. If affirmative, she is asked how prolonged the feelings were, how frequent, and the degree to which her activities, energy level, sleep, and concentration, were affected. To be classified as having a major depressive episode, a mother must report having had a two-week period in the preceding year during which she either experienced feeling sad, blue, or depressed or that she lost interest in things for at least most of the day almost every day. She also must report having had at least three other symptoms of major depression.

Table A.1 The Effects of Maternal Employment Patterns on Child Well-Being: Expanded Models

	Dependent variables—child outcomes$_t$				
	OLS			Probit models (marginal effects)	
Maternal employment-related variables	Behavior problem index$_t$ (1)	Externalizing scale$_t$ (2)	Internalizing scale$_t$ (3)	Prob(disruptive in school)$_t$ (4)	Prob(school absenteeism)$_t$ (5)
Years of work experience$_t$	−0.08**	−0.02**	−0.02	−0.00	−0.00
(ref cat: Job Stability)	(0.04)	(0.01)	(0.01)	(0.00)	(0.00)
Cumulative years of job instability$_{W0,t}$	0.45***	0.08*	0.15**	0.03**	0.03**
	(0.15)	(0.05)	(0.06)	(0.02)	(0.01)
Cumulative years of voluntary job mobility$_{W0,t}$	0.05	0.01	−0.01	−0.01	−0.02
	(0.21)	(0.07)	(0.09)	(0.02)	(0.02)
Cumulative years of full-time work$_{W0,t}$	−0.01	−0.03	−0.02	−0.01	0.01
	(0.12)	(0.04)	(0.05)	(0.01)	(0.01)
Cumulative years of fluctuating work hours$_{W0,t}$	0.21	0.09*	0.04	−0.01	0.02*
	(0.17)	(0.05)	(0.07)	(0.02)	(0.01)
Cumulative years used paid child care$_{W0,t}$	0.37**	0.04	0.17**	0.03	−0.04**
	(0.17)	(0.06)	(0.07)	(0.02)	(0.02)
Income sources and material hardship					
Net family income$_{t-1,t}$	−0.39**	−0.08	−0.19***	−0.01	−0.02
	(0.16)	(0.06)	(0.06)	(0.02)	(0.02)

Maternal labor earnings$_{t-1,t}$	0.34*	0.18***	0.06	0.05*	−0.00
	(0.20)	(0.07)	(0.08)	(0.02)	(0.03)
Received welfare$_{t-1,t}$	0.74***	0.30***	0.15	−0.01	0.04
	(0.26)	(0.09)	(0.10)	(0.03)	(0.04)
Food insufficiency index$_{t-1,t}$	1.19***	0.27***	0.55***	0.02	0.04
	(0.32)	(0.10)	(0.13)	(0.04)	(0.04)
Residential mobility/instability variables					
Moved$_{t-1,t}$	0.06	0.07	−0.01	0.04	−0.08***
	(0.23)	(0.08)	(0.09)	(0.03)	(0.03)
Moved$_{t-1,t}$*evicted$_{t-1,t}$	0.24	0.23	0.11	−0.04	0.06
	(0.42)	(0.15)	(0.17)	(0.05)	(0.05)
Neighborhood disadvantage (crime)$_{W1}$	0.46*	0.21**	0.01	0.01	−0.03
	(0.27)	(0.09)	(0.10)	(0.03)	(0.03)
Parental characteristics					
Parental stress index$_t$	0.10***	0.02**	0.03***	0.01***	−0.00
	(0.03)	(0.01)	(0.01)	(0.00)	(0.00)
Stressful life events index$_{W1}$	0.04	0.04	−0.01	−0.01	0.01
	(0.10)	(0.03)	(0.04)	(0.01)	(0.01)
Social support index$_{W1}$	−0.09	−0.02	−0.09	0.00	−0.00
	(0.15)	(0.05)	(0.06)	(0.01)	(0.01)
Maternal age$_t$	0.03	0.01	0.01	0.00	0.00
	(0.03)	(0.01)	(0.01)	(0.00)	(0.00)

(continued)

Table A.1 (continued)

	Dependent variables—child outcomes$_t$				
	Ols			Probit models (marginal effects)	
Maternal employment-related variables	Behavior problem index$_t$ (1)	Externalizing scale$_t$ (2)	Internalizing scale$_t$ (3)	Prob(disruptive in school)$_t$ (4)	Prob(school absenteeism)$_t$ (5)
Black (ref cat: white)	−0.88***	−0.11	−0.46***	0.06*	−0.02
	(0.30)	(0.10)	(0.11)	(0.03)	(0.03)
Maternal education (ref cat: HS dropout)					
HS grad$_t$	−0.08	−0.14	0.11	−0.03	−0.04
	(0.36)	(0.12)	(0.13)	(0.04)	(0.03)
Some college$_t$	−0.14	−0.30**	0.19	−0.00	−0.10***
	(0.38)	(0.12)	(0.14)	(0.04)	(0.04)
Home literacy environment index $_{W1}$	0.00	−0.01	0.03	0.02	−0.01
	(0.14)	(0.05)	(0.05)	(0.02)	(0.01)
Mom cohabiting$_{W1}$	−0.51	0.14	−0.21	0.09	−0.02
(ref cat: Married$_{W1}$)	(0.57)	(0.20)	(0.20)	(0.07)	(0.05)
Not cohabiting$_{W1}$	−0.05	0.08	−0.04	0.08	0.03
	(0.50)	(0.17)	(0.18)	(0.06)	(0.05)
Father involvement index$_{W1}$	−0.01	−0.01	−0.00	−0.00	−0.00
	(0.03)	(0.01)	(0.01)	(0.00)	(0.00)
Grandmother lives in HH$_{W1}$	0.72	0.08	0.41*	−0.02	−0.05
	(0.52)	(0.16)	(0.21)	(0.07)	(0.05)
Harsh parenting index$_{W1}$	0.27***	0.11***	0.08**	0.02*	0.00
	(0.09)	(0.03)	(0.03)	(0.01)	(0.01)

Mother's alcohol or drug use problem$_{t-1,t}$	0.84**	0.17	0.45***	0.04	0.05
	(0.34)	(0.12)	(0.13)	(0.04)	(0.04)
Mother's physical health problem$_{t-1,t}$	0.71**	0.25**	0.14	0.05	0.06
	(0.34)	(0.11)	(0.13)	(0.04)	(0.04)
Mother's probable diagnosis major depression$_{t-1,t}$	0.58*	0.16	0.22*	0.07*	0.07*
	(0.31)	(0.10)	(0.13)	(0.04)	(0.04)
Boy	0.92***	0.23**	0.26**	0.16***	0.06*
	(0.30)	(0.10)	(0.11)	(0.03)	(0.03)
Child age	0.13**	−0.02	0.12***	0.02***	−0.00
	(0.06)	(0.02)	(0.02)	(0.01)	(0.01)
Number of children in household	−0.12	−0.01	−0.08*	−0.02	−0.01
	(0.11)	(0.04)	(0.04)	(0.01)	(0.01)
Child-year observations	1,550	1,661	1,656	1,615	1,055
Number of children	515	524	523	513	452

NOTE: ***p<0.01; **p<0.05; *p<0.10. In these analyses, the coefficient on "years of work experience" represents mothers working and experiencing job stability, relative to those who did not work. The coefficients on cumulative years of job instability and voluntary job mobility are in reference to job stability. So, for example, the coefficient on "cumulative years of job instability" indicates the change in children's behavior associated with an additional year of work experience in an unstable job relative to that work experience in a stable job. To understand the influence on children of the movement from nonwork to a year of work experience in an unstable job, one would sum the coefficients on "years of work experience" and "cumulative years of job instability." Because nearly all mothers worked at some point over the past year, the work versus nonworking comparison is less useful than is characterizing the nature and pattern of employment, and identifying differential effects in the type of maternal work involvement on child well-being. Robust standard errors in parentheses.

Table A.2 The Effects of Changes in Maternal Employment Patterns on Changes in Child Well-Being: Expanded Models

	First-difference models Dependent variables—Δ child outcomes$_{t-1,t}$				
Maternal employment-related variables	Δ Behavior problem index$_{t-1,t}$ (1)	Δ Externalizing scale$_{t-1,t}$ (2)	Δ Internalizing scale$_{t-1,t}$ (3)	Δ Prob (disruptive in school)$_{t-1,t}$ (4)	Δ Prob (school absenteeism)$_{t-1,t}$ (5)
Worked$_{t-1,t}$ (ref cat: job stability)	−0.55*	−0.25**	−0.18*	−0.02	−0.08
	(0.30)	(0.10)	(0.10)	(0.04)	(0.06)
Worked$_{t-1,t}$*job instability$_{t-1,t}$	0.59**	0.13*	0.20**	0.02	0.04
	(0.26)	(0.08)	(0.09)	(0.04)	(0.04)
Worked$_{t-1,t}$*vol job mobility$_{t-1,t}$	0.42	0.02	0.09	0.04	0.03
	(0.27)	(0.09)	(0.10)	(0.04)	(0.05)
Δ Full-time work hours$_{t-1,t}$	0.07	0.13*	0.04	0.01	0.04
	(0.23)	(0.07)	(0.08)	(0.03)	(0.04)
Δ Fluctuating work hours$_{t-1,t}$	0.50**	0.12*	0.17**	−0.03	0.03
	(0.23)	(0.07)	(0.08)	(0.03)	(0.05)
Used paid child care services$_{t-1,t}$	0.34	0.04	0.26***	−0.02	−0.07
	(0.23)	(0.07)	(0.08)	(0.03)	(0.04)
Income sources and material hardship					
Δ Net family income$_{t-1,t}$	−0.17	0.02	−0.20***	−0.01	−0.04
	(0.17)	(0.09)	(0.07)	(0.02)	(0.03)
Δ Maternal labor earnings$_{t-1,t}$	0.34*	0.07	0.15*	0.07**	0.04
	(0.20)	(0.06)	(0.08)	(0.03)	(0.03)

Δ Received welfare$_{t-1,t}$	0.30	0.09	0.15*	-0.00	0.12**
	(0.25)	(0.08)	(0.08)	(0.04)	(0.05)
Δ Food insufficiency index$_{t-1,t}$	0.94***	0.15*	0.31***	0.00	0.04
	(0.29)	(0.08)	(0.10)	(0.04)	(0.04)
Residential mobility/instability variables					
Moved$_{t-1,t}$	−0.12	0.02	0.02	0.02	−0.08*
	(0.22)	(0.07)	(0.08)	(0.03)	(0.04)
Moved$_{t-1,t}$ *evicted$_{t-1,t}$	0.75**	0.26*	0.26**	−0.02	0.06
	(0.38)	(0.14)	(0.13)	(0.06)	(0.08)
Moved$_{t-1,t}$ *became homeowner$_{t-1,t}$	−0.04	0.07	−0.13	−0.09	0.04
	(0.38)	(0.12)	(0.14)	(0.06)	(0.05)
Moved$_{t-1,t}$ * Δ neighborhood poverty rate$_{t-1,t}$	−0.47	−0.12	0.17	0.04	0.12
	(1.01)	(0.36)	(0.40)	(0.20)	(0.24)
Demographic variables					
Pregnant$_{t-1,t}$	1.18**	0.02	0.56***	0.20***	0.09
	(0.55)	(0.16)	(0.19)	(0.07)	(0.11)
Father involvement index$_{W1}$	−0.01	0.00	0.01	0.00	−0.01***
	(0.02)	(0.01)	(0.01)	(0.00)	(0.00)
Δ Father involvement index$_{W1,W2}$	−0.02	0.00	−0.02	0.00	0.00
	(0.04)	(0.01)	(0.01)	(0.00)	(0.01)
Δ Grandmother lives in household$_{t-1,t}$	1.24*	0.42**	0.16	−0.07	0.09
	(0.65)	(0.18)	(0.20)	(0.11)	(0.21)
Δ Cohabiting$_{t-1,t}$ (ref cat: married)	0.96**	0.26**	0.27*	−0.09	0.06
	(0.40)	(0.13)	(0.16)	(0.06)	(0.08)

(continued)

Table A.2 (continued)

	First-difference models Dependent variables—Δ child outcomes$_{t-1,t}$				
	Δ Behavior problem index$_{t-1,t}$ (1)	Δ Externalizing scale$_{t-1,t}$ (2)	Δ Internalizing scale$_{t-1,t}$ (3)	Δ Prob (disruptive in school)$_{t-1,t}$ (4)	Δ Prob(school absenteeism)$_{t-1,t}$ (5)
Δ Not cohabiting$_{t-1,t}$	0.77*	0.08	0.25*	−0.06	0.03
	(0.43)	(0.13)	(0.15)	(0.06)	(0.09)
Maternal Health-related variables					
Δ Parental stress index$_{t-1,t}$	0.14***	0.04***	0.04***	0.01*	0.00
	(0.03)	(0.01)	(0.01)	(0.00)	(0.00)
Δ Mother's alcohol or drug use problem$_{t-1,t}$	0.72***	0.16	0.31***	0.06	−0.03
	(0.27)	(0.10)	(0.10)	(0.04)	(0.06)
Δ Mother's probable diagnosis major depression$_{t-1,t}$	−0.10	0.04	0.08	0.01	0.06
	(0.25)	(0.08)	(0.10)	(0.04)	(0.05)
Δ Mother's physical heath problem$_{t-1,t}$	0.34	0.05	0.19*	0.05	0.05
	(0.29)	(0.09)	(0.11)	(0.04)	(0.06)
Constant	0.69	0.38***	0.39***	0.15**	0.05
	(0.49)	(0.14)	(0.15)	(0.06)	(0.30)
Child-specific fixed effects?	First-difference form				
Child-year observations	1,045	1,663	1,653	1,476	742
Number of children	457	524	523	497	407

NOTE: All models include controls for changes in child age, maternal education, and home literacy environment scale. These effects are suppressed in the table to conserve space. Robust standard errors in parentheses (clustered on child). ***p<0.01; **p<0.05; *p<0.10.

Table A.3 The Longer-Run Impacts of Maternal Employment Patterns on Child Well-Being: Expanded Models

	Dependent variables—Δ child outcomes$_{W1,W5}$						
	Behavior problem index$_{W5}$ (1)	Externalizing scale$_{w5}$ (2)	Internalizing scale$_{w5}$ (3)	Prob (disruptive in school)$_{w5}$ (4)	Prob(school absenteeism)$_{w5}$ (5)	Prob(ever repeated a grade)$_{W3\text{-}W5}$ (6)	Prob(ever placed in special ed.)$_{W3\text{-}W5}$ (7)
Externalizing behavior subscale measure at *W1*	0.97***	1.54***					
	(0.21)	(0.25)					
Internalizing behavior subscale measure at *W1*	0.66**		1.17***				
	(0.27)		(0.24)				
Disruptive in school at *W1*				0.14*			
				(0.08)			
Maternal employment-related variables							
Δ no. of months worked$_{W1,W5}$	0.01	−0.01	0.00	0.00	0.00	0.00*	0.00
	(0.03)	(0.04)	(0.03)	(0.00)	(0.00)	(0.00)	(0.00)
Δ no. of invol. job-to-nonemployment transitions$_{W1,W5}$	1.00**	1.25**	1.29***	0.12**	0.00	0.03	0.03
	(0.41)	(0.54)	(0.39)	(0.05)	(0.03)	(0.03)	(0.02)
Δ no. of vol. job-to-nonemployment transitions$_{W1,W5}$	0.29	0.43	0.21	0.04	0.02	0.05***	0.00
	(0.20)	(0.27)	(0.19)	(0.02)	(0.02)	(0.02)	(0.01)
Δ no. of vol. job-to-job transitions$_{W1,W5}$	0.05	0.04	0.18	−0.03	−0.01	−0.02	−0.03*
	(0.27)	(0.35)	(0.26)	(0.03)	(0.02)	(0.02)	(0.02)
Δ Full-time work hours$_{W1,W5}$	0.99**	0.89	0.72*	0.02	0.03	0.06*	0.07**
	(0.44)	(0.58)	(0.42)	(0.05)	(0.04)	(0.04)	(0.03)

(continued)

Table A.3 (continued)

	Dependent variables—Δ child outcomes$_{W1,W5}$						
	Behavior problem index$_{W5}$ (1)	Externalizing scale$_{W5}$ (2)	Internalizing scale$_{W5}$ (3)	Prob (disruptive in school)$_{W5}$ (4)	Prob(school absenteeism)$_{W5}$ (5)	Prob(ever repeated a grade)$_{W3\text{-}W5}$ (6)	Prob(ever placed in special ed.)$_{W3\text{-}W5}$ (7)
Δ Full-time work hours$_{W1,W5}$*reading/writing/computer use	−0.93	−1.00	−0.14	−0.09	−0.09*	−0.04	−0.04
	(0.68)	(0.89)	(0.65)	(0.08)	(0.05)	(0.05)	(0.04)
Δ No. of yrs. spent working fluctuating hours$_{W1,W5}$	0.72***	0.73**	0.72***	−0.02	0.06***	0.04*	0.03
	(0.27)	(0.36)	(0.27)	(0.03)	(0.02)	(0.02)	(0.02)
Δ No. of yrs. used paid child care service$_{W1,W5}$ (for any child)	0.32	0.55*	0.69***	0.02	−0.02	0.00	0.06***
	(0.25)	(0.33)	(0.24)	(0.03)	(0.02)	(0.02)	(0.01)
Income sources and material hardship							
Δ Net family income$_{W1,W5}$	−0.22	−0.55	−0.11	−0.03	0.03	0.00	−0.03
	(0.27)	(0.36)	(0.26)	(0.03)	(0.02)	(0.02)	(0.02)
Δ Maternal labor earnings$_{W1,W5}$	0.20	0.80	−0.08	0.08*	−0.03	−0.01	−0.02
	(0.38)	(0.49)	(0.36)	(0.05)	(0.03)	(0.03)	(0.03)
Δ No. of yrs. received welfare$_{W1,W5}$	0.40	0.70**	0.24	0.02	−0.02	−0.01	0.00
	(0.25)	(0.33)	(0.24)	(0.03)	(0.02)	(0.02)	(0.02)
Δ No. of yrs. food insufficiency$_{W1,W5}$	0.69**	1.08***	0.53**	0.09***	0.02	0.02	0.01
	(0.27)	(0.35)	(0.26)	(0.03)	(0.02)	(0.02)	(0.01)

Residential mobility/ instability variables							
$Moved_{W1,W5}$	0.13	0.22	0.23	0.05*	0.00	0.02	−0.01
	(0.23)	(0.31)	(0.22)	(0.03)	(0.02)	(0.02)	(0.01)
$Moved_{W1,W5}$*$Evicted_{W1,W5}$	−0.32	−1.38	−0.15	−0.11	0.06	−0.06	0.03
	(0.82)	(1.08)	(0.79)	(0.09)	(0.07)	(0.05)	(0.05)
$Moved_{W1,W5}$* became $homeowner_{W1,W5}$	1.20*	2.04**	0.75	−0.01	0.00	−0.02	0.01
	(0.61)	(0.81)	(0.58)	(0.07)	(0.05)	(0.05)	(0.04)
$Moved_{W1,W5}$* Δ neighborhood poverty $rate_{W1,W5}$	−0.39	−1.98	0.24	−0.20	0.23	−0.07	−0.09
	(2.03)	(2.68)	(1.93)	(0.24)	(0.17)	(0.17)	(0.12)
Maternal Health-related variables							
Δ Mother's alcohol or drug use $problem_{W1,W5}$	−0.05	−0.83	−0.37	0.11	0.01	0.00	0.07*
	(0.60)	(0.79)	(0.58)	(0.08)	(0.05)	(0.05)	(0.04)
Δ Mother's probable diagnosis major $depression_{W1,W5}$	1.15**	1.27*	0.62	0.08	0.06	0.05	−0.07**
	(0.57)	(0.77)	(0.54)	(0.06)	(0.04)	(0.04)	(0.03)
Δ Mother's physical heath $problem_{W1,W5}$	−0.28	0.72	0.02	0.07	−0.05	0.01	0.00
	(0.58)	(0.75)	(0.55)	(0.07)	(0.04)	(0.04)	(0.03)
Two-year average transition probability (conditional on not occurring in prior periods)	—	—	—	—	—	0.1254	0.1381
Number of children	279	277	277	297	359	331	337

NOTE: ***p<0.01; **p<0.05; *p<0.10. All models include a constant and controls for gender, child age, and changes in maternal education, home literacy environment scale, family structure, father involvement in child rearing, and whether worked between waves. These effects are suppressed in the table to conserve space. Robust standard errors in parentheses.

Table A.4 Unconditional Growth Curve Models of Children's Behavioral Problems

	Hierarchical random effects models—dependent variables		
	Behavior problem index (1)	Externalizing behavior problems (2)	Internalizing behavior problems (3)
Boy	0.8956***	0.2669***	0.0136
	(0.3090)	(0.0938)	(0.0943)
Mean growth rate, $\beta 10$, (years since wave 1)	0.1419***	−0.0316**	0.1424***
	(0.0415)	(0.0125)	(0.0163)
Mean initial score, 1997, β00	15.9784***	4.6067***	5.7616***
	(0.2384)	(0.0701)	(0.0674)
Random effects components			
SD(random intercept)	3.2312***	1.0358***	0.8423***
	(0.1732)	(0.0451)	(0.0499)
SD(random coef on age)	0.4490***	0.1440***	0.2241***
	(0.0566)	(0.0170)	(0.0190)
Corr(initial level, growth rate)	−0.1971*	−0.2682**	0.3407**
	(0.1135)	(0.0906)	(0.1293)
SD(transitory component)	2.2527***	0.9296***	1.0536***
	(0.0598)	(0.0906)	(0.0213)
Child-year observations	1570	2253	2246
Number of children	518	575	575

NOTE: ***p<0.01; **p<0.05; *p<0.10. Robust standard errors in parentheses.

Appendix B
Empirical Methods

Child development is a complex process, with maternal work patterns representing only one influence on how children develop. Because of the inherently dynamic character of children's development, an outcome in one period is influenced by outcomes in earlier periods and inputs—from the home and other environments. The use of longitudinal data is necessary to address these issues. Our approach, which relies on rich, longitudinal data, has several advantages.

The empirical framework we adopt for the estimation of a child well-being production function conceptualizes child development as a cumulative process. The current and past inputs from maternal and other investments interact with the child's innate ability to produce child development. The child well-being production function is shown in Equation (B.1):

$$\text{(B.1)} \quad O_{it} = \beta_1 T_{it} + \beta_2 C_{it} + \beta_3 G_{it} + \beta_4 X_{it} + \alpha_i + v_{it} \,,$$

where O_{it} is a behavioral outcome for child i at age t; T_{it} is a measure of the quantity/quality of maternal time spent with the child through age t; C_{it} is a measure for the quantity/quality of child care and other nonmaternal time inputs; G_{it} represents goods used in the production of child development (e.g., financial investments in medical care and books/toys to promote healthy child development); X_{it} is a vector of controls for living arrangements, parental characteristics, and demographic variables. The error component, α_i, represents a fixed innate child ability/temperament effect, and v_{it} is a transitory error term that may be interpreted as a measurement error in the reported child behavioral outcome.

EMPIRICAL STRATEGY

The primary methodological challenge in estimating the impact of maternal labor supply and employment patterns on child well-being stems from the fact that the decision to work or stay at home (or the choice of the type of work and number of work hours more generally) is endogenous to child outcomes. Moreover, mothers who hold jobs, work long hours, or experience a given type of job transition, for example, differ from those who do not in both observable and unobservable ways that may also affect child well-being. As a result, cross-sectional estimates of the impact of hours worked by the mother on measures of child well-being may suffer from both simultaneity and omitted variable bias (due to unobserved heterogeneity). For example, children with mothers who experience job stability may come from relatively more advantaged family backgrounds and possess attributes that promote positive child development outcomes. Similarly, mothers may vary their work hours in response to a perceived need to provide greater supervision to certain children (i.e., reverse causality). Most prior analyses inadequately control for this heterogeneity and therefore may substantially understate the costs of maternal employment.

To address these issues we estimate the following models: 1) OLS models; 2) child fixed effects (specified in first-difference form); and 3) longer-run value-added fixed-effects models. We examine the influence on children of the level of work intensity (work hours) as well as the influence of the volatility of maternal work patterns. In our primary models, we exclude arguably endogenous variables and factors that *result* from maternal job-holding (such as family income, parental stress, housing and neighborhood conditions), since these capture a portion of the labor supply effect. To assess the role of such time-varying factors, we then examine how our estimates of the effects of maternal work patterns are influenced by the inclusion of an extensive set of time-varying covariates in the models. In this approach, we follow Altonji, Elder, and Taber (2005), Duncan (2003), and Ruhm (2004), who gauge how sensitive maternal employment effect estimates are to selection on unobservable variables by using the degree of selection on observables as a guide. The comparison of estimated coefficients on maternal employment patterns that result from standard and expanded models also enable us to examine the extent that the impacts of maternal employment patterns operate through these other factors. Large changes in estimates of the effect of maternal employment between the standard and expanded model specifications suggest significant selection on observable variables, and by extension, imply that there may be significant selection on unobserved variables; while small changes in estimated effects suggest only a minor role for potential selection bias. We outline in more detail below the three empirical approaches that we take.

Ordinary Least Squares Models

The main OLS model we estimate may be specified as

$$\text{(B.2)} \quad O_{it} = \alpha_0 + \beta E_{it}^{m} + \delta X_{it}^{p} + \varphi X_{it}^{c} + \varepsilon_{it} ,$$

where O represents child outcome measure for child i at time t; E represents a vector of maternal cumulative employment pattern measures experienced through time t (e.g., total years of work experience; cumulative number of years the mother experienced job stability, instability, and job mobility, respectively; cumulative number of years worked full time and fluctuating hours, respectively [since originally observed on the welfare rolls in February 1997]). X^p and X^c are vectors of parents' (p) and children's (c) demographic characteristics, including child age, gender, race, maternal age and education, home literacy environment scale, family structure, living arrangements, and the extent of father involvement in child rearing; and ε represents the composite error term, including permanent (α_i) and transitory components (v_{it}). For the child outcomes that are binary indicators—whether the child had school absenteeism problems and whether the child exhibited disobedient or disruptive behavior problems in school—we estimate probit models and present the marginal effects evaluated at the means. Linear probability models for these latter outcomes yielded the same pattern of results.

Fixed-Effects Models

Our primary method involves the estimation of child fixed effects (CFE) models (specified in first-difference form as discussed below), taking advantage of the repeated measures of child well-being and maternal work behavior over time. This estimation strategy identifies changes in child outcomes for an individual child over time as a function of changes in maternal employment patterns, controlling for common age-related development effects. This approach will successfully control for all observable and unobservable family and child characteristics that do not change over time.

Equations (B.3) and (B.4) represent two observations, one at time $t-1$ and the other at time t, for the same child.

$$\text{(B.3)} \quad O_{i(t-1)} = \alpha_0 + \alpha_i + \beta E^m_{i(t-1)} + \delta X^p_{i(t-1)} + \varphi X^c_{i(t-1)} + v_{i(t-1)}$$

$$\text{(B.4)} \quad O_{it} = \alpha_0 + \alpha_i + \beta E^m_{it} + \delta X^p_{it} + \varphi X^c_{it} + v_{it}$$

The term α_i represents the child-specific fixed effect. Parental characteristics are allowed to change over time although some of them may remain constant. Based on these equations, we estimate a model of changes in child outcomes of the form

$$\text{(B.5)} \quad \Delta O^c_{it} = \beta * \Delta E^m_{it} + \delta * \Delta X^p_{it} + \varphi * \Delta X^c_{it} + \Delta v^c_{it} \ ,$$

where all differences are estimated by subtracting characteristics of the previous time period from those of the contemporaneous period. The advantage of this model is that all observable and unobservable family- and child-specific fixed effects are differenced out. The effect is identified from the difference in children's outcomes as a function of maternal employment patterns experienced over the past one to two years (job stability, voluntary job-to-job changes, and involuntary job instability), changes in work hours, and other changes in job attributes that have occurred over this period.[2] This model is also sufficiently flexible to control for observable differences in family characteristics that have taken place over time.

One disadvantage of the CFE model is that it does not control for unobservable family characteristics that change over time. Maternal job changes may be associated with other stressful life events. That is, there might be changes within the family (or for the child) that coincide with differences in maternal employment characteristics that also impact the child's outcomes. Our expanded model specifications that include the more extensive set of observable maternal and family characteristics aim to assess the role of these potential sources of bias and minimize their influence. However, if unobserved maternal characteristics are associated with patterns of employment continuity and children's developmental trajectories, then our child differenced-based estimates of the effect of maternal employment would be biased.

Long-Difference Models

A well-known drawback with any difference method is that it may exacerbate attenuation bias due to measurement error (Greene 1993). For this reason we have chosen to estimate child fixed-effect models in long differences in addition to the primary first difference specifications described above. If a mother's work behavior is highly serially correlated, then much of the observed variation in work intensity over short periods of time may be due to measurement error. Long differences reduce this problem (Griliches and Hausman 1986). An additional consideration is that fixed-effect estimation is not always precise enough to distinguish between some potentially large effects from effects that are essentially equal to zero. Some previous work, using small and unrepresentative samples, have often inappropriately interpreted large and imprecisely estimated coefficients as indicating no effect, without consideration of statistical power.

The long-difference specifications are designed to examine the longer-run impacts of maternal employment patterns on child development, and to investigate whether these effects compound over time. By comparing the results of first-difference and long-difference fixed-effects models, we examine whether the influence of maternal work behavior on child behavioral outcomes represents a short-term adjustment, or whether employment effects have longer-run consequences for child well-being.

We estimate a longer-run model of changes in child outcomes of the form shown in Equation (B.6). In particular, we use as dependent variables child outcomes measured at the end of the sample period, and use cumulative measures of maternal employment spanning the period between the first and last waves to predict these outcomes. We do this while controlling for the corresponding child assessment measure from the first wave, so coefficient estimates on the maternal employment pattern variables over the subsequent six-year period can be interpreted as the cumulative effects of these employment patterns on the change in child well-being over the sample period.

$$\text{(B.6)} \quad O_{i5} = \alpha_0 + \alpha O_{i1} + \beta E^{m}_{i,\Delta 1-5} + \delta X^{p}_{i,\Delta 1-5} + \varphi X^{c}_{i,\Delta 1-5} + v_{i5}$$

We count the total number of times during these five waves that a mother experienced long work hours, job instability, or unpredictable work hours, and then ask whether the total number of periods a child's mother experienced a given job condition (for example, long hours) predicts changes during that same five years in children's behavior. This allows us to examine the cumulative effect of mothers' work on children's behavior, rather than simply the effect occurring in one period, as in the child fixed-effects model.

As discussed in Chapter 2, we examine self-reports for reasons of job separations to ensure that our estimated effects of job instability are not driven by mother's response to a perceived need to provide supervision and care for the child. We also perform some analyses separately for involuntary job losses due to being fired/laid-off when this information is available. There is some noncomparability in the characterization of involuntary job loss (i.e., being fired/laid off) because of changes in the wording of these questions across waves, so we emphasize the involuntary job loss effects in the longer-run models as opposed to the short-run models that use between-wave changes that could instead reflect changes in the wording of the survey question.

We expect school-related academic progress indicators such as grade repetition and placement in special education to be more sensitive to persistent exposure to working conditions over several years as opposed to exposures that occur in a single period. We therefore analyze the longer-run impacts of maternal employment patterns experienced between 1997 and 2003 on the likelihood of grade repetition and placement in special education by the end of the sample period, conditional on these transitions not occurring in previous periods. We estimate the impact of the cumulative maternal employment experiences over the wave 1 to wave 5 period on the transition probabilities for these outcomes between waves 3 and 5 to help ensure that the maternal employment pattern preceded the assessed child outcome. Thus, for the longer-run models, we estimate probit models of whether the child repeated a grade between waves 3 through 5 and whether the child had been placed in special education, conditional on the child not repeating a grade or being placed in special education in any previous period. We present the marginal effects on the likelihood of these probabilities, evaluated at the means of the set of explanatory measures.

Finally, we also use our longer-run models to predict child behavioral outcomes and academic progress indicators at the end of the study using the low-, medium-, and high-profile maternal work patterns experienced over the 1997–2003 period (as defined in Chapter 2), after controlling for the initial child outcome measure at wave 1, child age, gender, race, maternal age and education, home literacy, family structure, and living arrangements.

Notes

1. In alternative model specifications (not shown), we examined whether children are more affected by the onset of long maternal work hours (or volatility of work patterns) in the contemporaneous period in which it occurs, or whether effects manifest in subsequent periods. The results provided some indication that maternal employment patterns in the recent 12 months may be more important than employment patterns at other times. For example, an additional year of exposure to maternal fluctuating work hours during the child's life is related to approximately a 0.26 (0.09) point higher behavior problem index (externalizing) score; if that additional volatility in maternal work hours from week-to-week results from a change in work hours status that occurred over the most recent year, the estimated increase in the behavior problem index (externalizing scale) is an additional 0.38 (0.15). Thus, the strength of the total estimated relationship between children's recent exposure to fluctuating work hours and behavior problems is equivalent to 27 percent of a standard deviation increase in the behavior problem index.
2. Our job transition pattern variables are flow measures between waves, while our work hours variables are stock measures (e.g., whether she had fluctuating work hours on her most recent job and whether the job was full time). Accordingly, the difference specification for the job transition pattern measures represent whether a mother experienced an additional year of job instability (relative to job stability), while the difference specification for the work hours variables represent whether there was a change in full-time job status and fluctuating (versus regular) work schedules. In this way, the maternal employment variables we include are all specified in difference form (i.e., change in hours status and change in cumulative number of periods mother experienced relevant job transition type); the differencing also eliminates time-invariant unobserved child heterogeneity.

References

Abidin, Richard R. 1990. *Index Short Form: Test Manual.* University of Virginia. (36-item version).

Acs, Gregory, and Pamela Loprest. 2004. *Leaving Welfare: Employment and Well-Being of Families That Left Welfare in the Post-Entitlement Era.* Kalamazoo, MI: W.E. Upjohn Institute for Employment Research.

Adam, Emma, and Lindsay Chase-Lansdale. 2002. "Home Sweet Home(s): Parental Separations, Residential Moves, and Adjustment Problems in Low-Income Adolescent Girls." *Developmental Psychology* 38(5): 792–805.

Allard, Scott, Rucker C. Johnson, and Sheldon Danziger. 2007. "Residential Mobility among Low-Income Women after Welfare Reform." UC-Berkeley working paper. Berkeley, CA: University of California. http://istsocrates.berkeley.edu/~ruckerj/abstract_residentialmobilityafterwelfare_9-07.pdf (accessed April 15, 2009).

Altonji, Joseph, Todd Elder, and Christopher Taber. 2005. "Selection on Observed and Unobserved Variables: Assessing the Effectiveness of Catholic Schools." *Journal of Political Economy* 113(1): 151–184.

Anderson, Nathaniel, and Kristin S. Seefeldt. 2000. "Inside Michigan Work First Programs." Ann Arbor, MI: Michigan Program on Poverty and Social Welfare Policy.

Baker, Paula C., Canada K. Keck, Frank L. Mott, and Stephen V. Quinlan. 1993. *NLSY Child Handbook: A Guide to the 1986–1990 National Longitudinal Survey of Youth Child Data.* Rev. ed. Columbus, OH: Center for Human Resource Research, Ohio State University.

Bane, Mary Jo. 1997. "Welfare as We Might Know It." *American Prospect* 30: 47–53. http://www.prospect.org/cs/articles?article=welfare_as_we_might_know_it_1197 (accessed April 15, 2009).

Bernstein, Jared, and Mark Greenberg. 2001. "Reforming Welfare Reform." *American Prospect* (Web only). http://www.prospect.org/cs/articles?article=reforming_welfare_reform_010101 (accessed January 30, 2009).

Bianchi, Suzanne. 2000. "Maternal Employment and Time with Children: Dramatic Change or Surprising Continuity?" *Demography* 37(4): 401–414.

Bitler, Marianne, Jonah Gelbach, and Hilary Hoynes. 2006. "Welfare Reform and Children's Living Arrangements." *Journal of Human Resources* 41(1): 1–27.

Blair, Clancy. 2002. "School Readiness as Propensity for Engagement: Integrating Cognition and Emotion in a Neurobiological Conceptualization of Child Functioning at School Entry." *American Psychologist* 57: 111–127.

Blank, Rebecca M. 1998. *It Takes a Nation: A New Agenda for Fighting Poverty.* New York: Russell Sage.

Bloom, Dan, James J. Kemple, Pamela Morris, Susan Scrivener, Nandita Verma, Richard Hendra, Diana Adams-Ciardullo, David Seith, and Johanna Walter. 2000. *The Family Transition Program: Final Report on Florida's Initial Time-Limited Welfare Program*. New York: MDRC.

Bloom, Dan, Cindy Redcross, JoAnn Hsueh, Sarah Rich, and Vanessa Martin. 2007. *Four Strategies to Overcome Barriers to Employment: An Introduction to the Enhanced Services for the Hard-to-Employ Demonstration and Evaluation Project.* New York: MDRC.

Bloom, Dan, Susan Scrivener, Charles Michalopoulos, Pamela Morris, Richard Hendra, Diana Adams-Ciardullo, and Johanna Walter. 2002. *Jobs First Final Report on Connecticut's Welfare Reform Initiative*. New York: MDRC.

Bound, John, Charlie Brown, Greg J. Duncan, and Willard L. Rodgers. 1994. "Evidence on the Validity of Cross-Sectional and Longitudinal Labor Market Data." *Journal of Labor Economics* 12(3): 345–368.

Brown, Susan. 2004. "Family Structure and Child Well-Being: The Significance of Parental Cohabitation." *Journal of Marriage and Family* 66(2): 351–367.

Bumpass, Larry, and Hsien-Hen Lu. 2000. "Trends in Cohabitation and Implications for Children's Family Context in the United States." *Population Studies* 54(1): 29–41.

Cadena, Brian, and Andreas Pape. 2006. "How Does Attrition Affect the Women's Employment Study Data?" National Poverty Center, University of Michigan, Ann Arbor, MI. Photocopy.

Catalano, Ralph, D. Dooley, G. Wilson, and R. Hough. 1993. "Job Loss and Alcohol Abuse: A Test Using Data from the Epidemiologic Catchment Area Project." *Journal of Health and Social Behavior* 34(3): 215–225.

Center for Human Resource Research. 1993. *NLSY Child Handbook.* Columbus, OH: Center for Human Resource Research.

Chase-Lansdale, P. Lindsay, Robert A. Moffitt, Brenda J. Lohman, Andrew J. Cherlin, Rebekah Levine Coley, Laura D. Pittman, Jennifer Roff, and Elizabeth Votruba-drzal. 2003. "Mothers' Transitions from Welfare to Work and the Well-Being of Preschoolers and Adolescents." *Science* 299(5612): 1548–1552.

Chase-Lansdale, P. Lindsay, Frank L. Mott, Jeanne Brooks-Gunn, and Deborah A. Phillips. 1991. "Children of the NLSY: A Unique Research Opportunity." *Developmental Psychology* 27(6): 918–931.

Chatterji, Pinka, and Sara Markowitz. 2005. "Does the Length of Maternity Leave Affect Maternal Health?" *Southern Economic Journal* 72(1): 16–41.

Council of Economic Advisers. 1999. *The Effects of Welfare Policy and the Economic Expansion on Welfare Caseloads: An Update*. Technical report. Washington, DC: Council of Economic Advisers.

Crouse, Gil. 1999. "State Implementation of Major Changes to Welfare Policies, 1992–1998." Washington, DC: U.S. Department of Health and Human Services, Assistant Secretary for Planning and Evaluation.

Cunha, Flavio, and James Heckman. 2008. "Formulating, Identifying and Estimating the Technology of Cognitive and Non-cognitive Skill Formation." *Journal of Human Resources* 43(4): 738–782.

Currie, Janet, and Mark Stabile. 2006. "Child Mental health and Human Capital Accumulation: The Case of ADHD." *Journal of Health Economics* 25(6): 1094–1118.

Currie, Janet, and Wanchuan Lin. 2007. "Chipping Away at Health: More on the Relationship between Income and Child Health." *Health Affairs* 26(2): 331–344.

Danziger, Sandra, Mary Corcoran, Sheldon Danziger, Colleen Heflin, Ariel Kalil, Judith Levine, Daniel Rosen, Kristin Seefeldt, Kristine Siefert, and Richard Tolman. 2000. "Barriers to the Employment of Welfare Recipients." In *Prosperity for All,* R. Cherry and W.M. Rodgers, eds. New York: Russell Sage Foundation, pp. 245–278.

Danziger, Sheldon. 1997. "Welfare: Where Do We Go From Here?" *Atlantic online*. March 25. http://www.theatlantic.com/unbound/forum/welfare/danz3.htm (accessed April 15, 2009).

Danziger, Sheldon, Colleen Heflin, Mary Corcoran, Elizabeth Oltmans, and Hui-Chen Wang. 2002. "Does It Pay to Move from Welfare to Work?" *Journal of Policy Analysis and Management* 21(4): 671–692.

DeLeire, Thomas, and Ariel Kalil. 2002. "Good Things Come in 3's: Multigenerational Coresidence and Adolescent Adjustment." *Demography* 39: 393–413.

DeParle, Jason. 1994. "Mary Ann Moore's Welfare." *New York Times Sunday Magazine*. December 8, pp. 42–49.

———. 2004. *American Dream: Three Women, Ten Kids, and a Nation's Drive to End Welfare.* New York: Viking.

Devine, Carol M., Margaret Jastran, Jennifer A. Jabs, Elaine Wethington, Tracy J. Farrell, and Carole A. Bisogni. 2006. "A Lot of Sacrifices: Work-Family Spillover and the Food Choice Coping Strategies of Low Wage Employed Parents." *Social Science and Medicine* 63(10): 2591–2603.

Duncan, Greg J. 2003. "Modeling the Impacts of Child Care Quality on Children's Preschool Cognitive Development" (with the NICHD Early Child Care Research Network). *Child Development* 74(5): 1454–1475.

Duncan, Greg J., Aletha C. Huston, and Thomas Weisner. 2007. *Higher Ground: New Hope for the Working Poor and Their Children.* New York: Russell Sage Foundation.

Edelman, Peter. 1997. "Opening Statements." *Atlantic online*. March 25. http://

www.theatlantic.com/unbound/forum/welfare/intro.htm (accessed April 15, 2009).

Edin, Kathryn, and Maria Kefalas. 2005. *Promises I Can Keep: Why Poor Women Put Motherhood before Marriage.* Berkeley: University of California Press.

Ellwood, David T. 1988. *Poor Support: Poverty in the American Family.* New York: Basic Books.

Ellwood, David T., and Frances Fox Piven. 1996. "Was Welfare Reform Worthwhile?" *American Prospect* 27: 14. http://www.prospect.org/cs/articles?article=was_welfare_reform_worthwhile (accessed April 20, 2009).

Fiese, Barbara H., Thomas J. Tomcho, Michael Douglas, Kimberly Josephs, Scott Poltrock, and Tim Baker. 2002. "A Review of 50 Years of Research on Naturally Occurring Family Routines and Rituals: Cause for Celebration?" *Journal of Family Psychology* 16(4): 381–390.

Gennetian, Lisa, Leonard Lopoo, and Andrew London. 2008. "Maternal Work Hours and Adolescents' School Outcomes among Low-Income Families in Four Urban Countries." *Demography* 45(1): 31–53.

Gennetian, Lisa, and Cynthia Miller. 2002. "Children and Welfare Reform: A View from an Experimental Welfare Program in Minnesota." *Child Development* 73(2): 601–620.

Gladden, Tricia, and Christopher Taber. 2000. "Wage Progression among Less-Skilled Workers." In *Finding Jobs: Work and Welfare Reform,* David Card and Rebecca M. Blank, eds. New York: Russell Sage Foundation, pp. 160–192.

Greene, William. 1993. *Econometric Analysis.* 2nd ed. Upper Saddle River, New Jersey: Prentice-Hall.

Griliches, Zvi, and Jerry Hausman. 1986. "Errors in Variables in Panel Data." *Journal of Econometrics* 31(1): 93–118.

Hanushek, Eric A., John F. Kain, and Steven G. Rivkin. 2004. "Disruption versus Tiebout Improvement: The Costs and Benefits of Switching Schools." *Journal of Public Economics* 88: 1721–1746.

Haskins, Ron. 2006. *Work over Welfare: The Inside Story of the 1996 Welfare Reform Law.* Washington, DC: Brookings Institution Press.

Haveman, Robert, and Barbara Wolfe. 1995. "The Determinants of Children's Attainments: A Review of Methods and Findings." *Journal of Economic Literature* 33(3): 1829–1878.

Heckman, James, Robert Lalonde, and Jeffrey Smith. 1999. "The Economics and Econometrics of Active Labor Market Programs." In *Handbook of Labor Economics: Volume 3A,* Orley Ashenfelter and David Card, eds. Amsterdam: Elsevier Science, pp. 1865–2097.

Henly, Julia R., and Susan Lambert. 2005. "Nonstandard Work and Child Care Needs of Low-Income Parents." In *Work, Family, Health, and Well-Being,* S.M. Bianchi, L.M. Casper, and R.B. King, eds. Mahwah, NJ: Erlbaum, pp. 473–492.

Henly, Julia.R., H. Luke Shaefer, and Elaine Waxman. 2006. "Nonstandard Work Schedules: Employer- and Employee-Driven Flexibility in Retail Jobs." *Social Service Review* 80(4): 609–634.

Hochschild, Arlie Russell. 1989. *The Second Shift: Working Parents and the Revolution at Home.* New York: Viking.

Holt, Steve. 2006. *The Earned Income Tax Credit at 30: What We Know.* Washington, DC: Brookings Institution.

Holzer, Harry J., and Robert J. LaLonde. 2000. "Job Change and Job Stability among Less Skilled Young Workers." In *Finding Jobs: Work and Welfare Reform,* David Card and Rebecca M. Blank, eds. New York: Russell Sage Foundation, pp. 125–159.

Holzer, Harry J., and Karin Martinson. 2008. "Helping Poor Working Parents Get Ahead: Federal Funds for New State Strategies and Systems." New Safety Net Paper no. 4. Washington, DC: Urban Institute.

Hotz, V. Joseph, Guido W. Imbens, and Jacob A. Klerman. 2006. "Evaluating the Differential Effects of Alternative Welfare-to-Work Training Components: A Re-analysis of the California GAIN Program." *Journal of Labor Economics* 24(3): 521–566.

Huston, Aletha C., Greg J. Duncan, Robert Granger, Johannes Bos, Vonnie McLoyd, Mistry Rashmita, Danielle Crosby, Christina Gibson, Katherine Magnuson, Jennifer Romich, and Ana Ventura. 2001. "Work-Based Antipoverty Programs for Parents Can Enhance the School Performance and Social Behavior of Children." *Child Development* 72(1): 318–336.

Ingersoll, Gary M., James P. Scamman, and Wayne D. Eckerling. 1989. "Geographic Mobility and Student Achievement in an Urban Setting." *Educational Evaluation and Policy Analysis* 11(2): 143–149.

Jencks, Christopher. 2005. "1990: Welfare Then and Now." *American Prospect.* http://www.prospect.org/cs/articles?article=1990_welfare_then_and_now (accessed April 20, 2009).

Jencks, Christopher, Scott Winship, and Joseph Swingle. 2006. "Welfare Redux." *American Prospect* 17(3): 36–40. http://www.prospect.org/cs/articles?article=welfare_redux (accessed January 30, 2009).

Johnson, Rucker C. 2006. "Wage and Job Dynamics after Welfare Reform: The Importance of Job Skills." *Research in Labor Economics* 26: 231–298.

Johnson, Rucker C., and Mary Corcoran. 2003. "The Road to Economic Self-Sufficiency: Job Quality and Job Transition Patterns after Welfare Reform." *Journal of Public Policy Analysis and Management* 22(4): 615–639.

Joshi, Pamela, and Karen Bogen. 2007. "Nonstandard Schedules and Young Children's Behavioral Outcomes among Working Low-Income Families." *Journal of Marriage and Family* 69(1): 139–156.

Kalil, Ariel, and Kathleen Ziol-Guest. 2005. "Single Mothers' Employment Dynamics and Adolescent Well-Being." *Child Development* 76(1): 196–211.

Kaus, Mickey. 1992. *The End of Equality.* 2nd ed. New York: Basic Books.

Kefalas, Maria. 2007. "Single Mama Drama." *Huffington Post,* May 9. http://www.huffingtonpost.com/maria-kefalas/single-mama-drama_b_48020.html (accessed April 20, 2009).

Kessler, Ronald C. 1997. "The Effects of Stressful Life Events on Depression." *Annual Review of Psychology* 48: 191–214.

Kessler, Ronald C., Katherine A. McGonagle, Shanyang Zhao, Christopher B. Nelson, Michael Hughes, Suzann Eshleman, Hans-Ulrich Wittchen, and Kenneth S. Kendler. 1994. "Lifetime and 12-Month Prevalence of DSM-III-R Psychiatric Disorders in the United States: Results from the National Comorbidity Survey." *Archives of General Psychiatry* 51(1): 8–19.

Kunz, James, and Ariel Kalil. 1999. "Self-Esteem, Self-Efficacy, and Welfare Use." *Social Work Research* 23(2): 119–126.

Lambert, Susan. 2009. "Making a Difference for Hourly Employees." In *Work-Life Policies That Make a Real Difference for Individuals, Families, and Communities,* Ann C. Crouter and Alan Booth, eds. Washington, DC: Urban Institute Press, pp. 169–193.

Leininger, Lindsey, and Ariel Kalil. 2008. "Cognitive and Non-Cognitive Predictors of Success in Adult Education Programs: Evidence from Experimental Data with Low-Income Welfare Recipients." *Journal of Policy Analysis and Management* 27(3): 521–535.

Lopoo, Leonard. 2007. "While the Cat's Away, Do the Mice Play? Maternal Employment and the After-School Activities of Adolescents." *Social Science Quarterly* 88(5): 1357–1373.

Lower-Basch, Elizabeth. 2007. *Opportunity at Work: Improving Job Quality.* CLASP policy paper, Opportunity at Work Series Paper no. 1. Washington, DC: Center for Law and Social Policy.

McLanahan, Sara, and Gary Sandefur. 1994. *Growing Up with a Single Parent: What Hurts, What Helps*. Cambridge, MA: Harvard University Press.

McLoyd, Vonnie, Toby Jayaratne, Rosario Ceballo, and Julio Borquez. 1994. "Unemployment and Work Interruption among African American Single Mothers: Effects on Parenting and Adolescent Socioemotional Functioning." *Child Development* 65(2): 562–589.

Michalopoulos, Charles, Christine Schwartz, and Diana Adams-Ciardullo. 2001. "What Works Best for Whom: Impacts of 20 Welfare-to-Work Programs by Subgroup." National Evaluation of Welfare-to-Work Strategies. New York: MDRC.

Michigan Program on Poverty and Social Welfare Policy. 2004. *The Women's Employment Study: A Brief Review of Findings from a Panel Survey of Current and Former Welfare Recipients.* Ann Arbor, MI: Gerald R. Ford School of Public Policy, University of Michigan. http://www.fordschool.umich.edu/research/pdf/weschartbook.pdf (accessed October 7, 2009).

Miller, Cynthia, Aletha C. Huston, Greg J. Duncan, Vonnie C. McLoyd, and Thomas S. Weisner. 2008. *New Hope for the Working Poor: Effects after Eight Years for Families and Children.* New York: MDRC.

Murray, Charles. 1984. *Losing Ground: American Social Policy, 1950–1980.* 2nd ed. New York: Basic Books.

National Governors Association. 2003. "MCH Update 2002: State Health Coverage for Low-Income Pregnant Women, Children, and Parents." Washington, DC: Nation Governors Association.

Newman, Katherine S. 2000. "On the High Wire: How the Working Poor Juggle Job and Family Responsibilities." In *Balancing Acts: Easing the Burdens and Improving the Options for Working Families,* E. Applebaum, ed. Washington DC: Economic Policy Institute, pp. 73–85.

Newman, Katherine S., and Victor Tan Chen. 2007. *The Missing Class: Portraits of the Near Poor in America.* New York: Beacon Press.

Newman, Katherine S., and Margaret M. Chin. 2002. "High Stakes, Hard Choices: When School Reformers Want Parents to Spend More Time on Homework and Welfare Reformers Demand More Time on the Job, What's Supposed to Give?" *American Prospect* 13(13). http://www.prospect.org/cs/articles?article=high_stakes_hard_choices (accessed April 20, 2009).

O'Leary, Christopher J., Robert A. Straits, and Stephen A. Wandner. 2004. "Public Job Training: Experience and Prospects." In *Job Training Policy in the United States*, Christopher J. O'Leary, Robert A. Straits, and Stephen A. Wandner, eds. Kalamazoo, MI: W.E. Upjohn Institute for Employment Research, pp. 289–310.

Parrott, Sharon, and Arloc Sherman. 2006. *TANF at 10: Program Results Are More Mixed than Often Understood.* Washington, DC: Center on Budget and Policy Priorities.

Pettit, Greg S., Robert D. Laird, John.E. Bates, and Kenneth A. Dodge. 1997. "Patterns of After-School Care in Middle Childhood: Risk Factors and Developmental Outcomes." *Merrill-Palmer Quarterly* 43(3): 552–538.

Piven, Frances Fox, Margaret Hallock, and Sandra Morgen, eds. 2002. *Work, Welfare and Politics: Confronting Poverty in the Wake of Welfare Reform.* Eugene, OR: University of Oregon Press.

Presser, Harriet. 2004. "Employment in a 24/7 Economy." In *Work-Family Challenges for Low-Income Parents and Their Children,* A. Crouter and A. Booth, eds. Mahwah, NJ: Erlbaum, pp. 83–106.

Presser, Harriet, and Amy Cox. 1997. "The Work Schedules of Low-Educated American Women and Welfare Reform." *Monthly Labor Review* 120(94): 25–34.

Rector, Robert. 1997. "The Future of Welfare: Where Do We Go from Here?" *Atlantic online*. Roundtable: Atlantic Unbound. http://www.theatlantic.com/unbound/forum/welfare/intro.htm (accessed April 20, 2009).

Roy, Kevin M., Carolyn Y. Tubbs, and Linda Burton. 2004. "'Don't Have No Time': Daily Rhythms and the Organization of Time for Low-Income Families." *Family Relations* 53(2): 168–178.

Royalty, Anne. 1998. "Job-to-Job and Job-to-Nonemployment Turnover by Gender and Education Level." *Journal of Labor Economics* 16(2): 392–443.

Ruhm, Christopher J. 2004. "Maternal Employment and Adolescent Development." NBER working paper no. 10691. Cambridge, MA: National Bureau of Economic Research.

Safire, William. 1997. *Lend Me Your Ears: Great Speeches in American History.* New York: W.W. Norton.

Schoeni, Robert, and Rebecca Blank. 2000. "What Has Welfare Reform Accomplished? Impacts on Welfare Participation, Employment, Income and Family Structure." NBER Working Paper No. 7627. Santa Monica, CA: RAND, Labor and Population Program.

Seefeldt, Kristin S. 2008. *Working after Welfare: How Women Balance Jobs and Family in the Wake of Welfare Reform.* Kalamazoo, MI: W.E. Upjohn Institute for Employment Research.

Seefeldt, Kristin S., LaDonna Pavetti, Karen Maguire, and Gretchen Kirby. 1998. *Income Support and Social Services for Low-Income People in Michigan.* Washington, DC: Urban Institute.

Seefeldt, Kristin S., Jacob Leos-Urbel, Patricia McMahon, and Kathleen Snyder. 2001. "Recent Changes in Michigan Welfare and Work, Child Care, and Child Welfare Systems." State Update No. 4. Washington, DC: Urban Institute.

Smolensky, Eugene, and Jennifer A. Gootman, eds. 2003. *Working Families and Growing Kids: Caring for Children and Adolescents.* Washington, DC: National Research Council and Institute of Medicine and National Academies Press.

Toner, Robin. 1995. "The 104th Congress: Welfare; Senate Approves Welfare Plan That Would End Aid Guarantee." *New York Times*, September 20, A:1.

Urban Institute. 2004. *Worst Case Sanctions.* Fast Facts. Washington, DC:

Urban Institute. http://www.urban.org/url.cfm?ID=900774 (accessed February 2, 2009).

U.S. Census Bureau. 2009. *Economic News Release.* Table 4. http://www.bls.gov/news.release/famee.t04.htm (accessed November 9, 2009).

———. n.d. *Detailed Poverty Tabulations from the CPS.* http://www.census.gov/hhs/www/poverty/detailedpovtabs.html (accessed July 29, 2009).

U.S. Department of Health and Human Services. 2007. *Indicators of Welfare Dependence Annual Report to Congress, 2007.* Appendix A, Table 10. http://www.aspe.hhs.gov/hsp/indicators07/apa.pdf (accessed April 20, 2009).

———. n.d. *Fact Sheet: What is TANF?* http://www.acf.hhs.gov/opa/fact_sheets/tanf_factsheet.html (accessed April 20, 2009).

U.S. Government Printing Office. 1997. Weekly Compilation of Presidential Documents. August 26. Washington, DC: GPO.

Waldfogel, Jane. 2009. "Family Policy as Anti-Poverty Policy." In *Changing Poverty,* Maria Cancian and Sheldon Danziger, eds. New York: Russell Sage Foundation, pp. 242–265.

Ware, John E., K. Snow, and Mark Kosinski. 1993. *SF-36 Health Survey: Manual and Interpretation Guide.* Boston, MA: Health Institute, New England Medical Center.

Weisner, Thomas S., Christina Gibson, Edward D. Lowe, and Jennifer Romich. 2002. "Understanding Working Poor Families in the New Hope Program." *Poverty Research Newsletter* 6(4): 3–5.

Wilson, William Julius. 1987. *The Truly Disadvantaged: The Inner City, the Underclass, and the Public Policy.* Chicago: University of Chicago Press.

Zaslow, Martha J., and Carolyn A. Eldred, eds. 1998. *Parenting Behavior in a Sample of Young Mothers in Poverty: Results of the New Chance Observational Study.* New York: MDRC.

Zedlewski, Sheila R., Pamela A. Holcomb, and Pamela J. Loprest. 2007. "Hard-to-Employ Parents: A Review of Their Characteristics and the Programs Designed to Serve Their Needs." *Low-Income Working Families,* No. 9. Washington, DC: Urban Institute.

The Authors

Rucker C. Johnson is an assistant professor in the Goldman School of Public Policy at the University of California, Berkeley. His graduate and postdoctoral training is in labor and health economics. His work considers the role of poverty and inequality in affecting life chances. He has focused on such topics as low-wage labor markets, spatial mismatch, the socioeconomic determinants of health disparities over the life course, and the effects of growing up poor and poor infant health on childhood cognition, child health, educational attainment, and later-life health and socioeconomic success.

Ariel Kalil is a professor in the Harris School of Public Policy Studies at the University of Chicago. Her graduate and postdoctoral training is in developmental psychology and public policy. Her work considers how economic conditions affect child well-being. Her prior studies have focused on such topics as parental job loss, poverty and income instability, teenage parenthood, and family structure.

Rachel E. Dunifon is an associate professor in the department of policy and management at Cornell University. Her graduate and postdoctoral training is in human development and public policy. Her work is in the area of child and family policy, focusing on issues such as the influence of family living arrangements on children, welfare reform and child well-being, and maternal work behavior and child development.

Index

The italic letters *f, n,* and *t* following a page number indicate that the subject information of the heading is within a figure, note, or table, respectively, on that page. Double italics indicate multiple but consecutive elements.

About the Institute

The W.E. Upjohn Institute for Employment Research is a nonprofit research organization devoted to finding and promoting solutions to employment-related problems at the national, state, and local levels. It is an activity of the W.E. Upjohn Unemployment Trustee Corporation, which was established in 1932 to administer a fund set aside by Dr. W.E. Upjohn, founder of The Upjohn Company, to seek ways to counteract the loss of employment income during economic downturns.

The Institute is funded largely by income from the W.E. Upjohn Unemployment Trust, supplemented by outside grants, contracts, and sales of publications. Activities of the Institute comprise the following elements: 1) a research program conducted by a resident staff of professional social scientists; 2) a competitive grant program, which expands and complements the internal research program by providing financial support to researchers outside the Institute; 3) a publications program, which provides the major vehicle for disseminating the research of staff and grantees, as well as other selected works in the field; and 4) an Employment Management Services division, which manages most of the publicly funded employment and training programs in the local area.

The broad objectives of the Institute's research, grant, and publication programs are to 1) promote scholarship and experimentation on issues of public and private employment and unemployment policy, and 2) make knowledge and scholarship relevant and useful to policymakers in their pursuit of solutions to employment and unemployment problems.

Current areas of concentration for these programs include causes, consequences, and measures to alleviate unemployment; social insurance and income maintenance programs; compensation; workforce quality; work arrangements; family labor issues; labor-management relations; and regional economic development and local labor markets.